THE
VICTORIAN
HOUSE
EXPLAINED

TREVOR YORKE

COUNTRYSIDE BOOKS
NEWBURY BERKSHIRE

First published 2005
© Trevor Yorke 2005
Reprinted 2007

COUNTRYSIDE BOOKS
3 Catherine Road
Newbury, Berkshire

To view our complete range of books,
please visit us at
www.countrysidebooks.co.uk

ISBN 1 85306 943 4
EAN 978185306 943 7

Photographs and illustrations by the author

Designed by Peter Davies, Nautilus Design

Produced through MRM Associates Ltd., Reading
Typeset by Techniset Typesetters, Newton-le-Willows
Printed by Cambridge University Press

CONTENTS

3

Introduction

R anging from the majestic rows of gleaming white Classical terraces in west London to the grid of violent red-brick houses in the Lancashire mill towns; and from the steeply pointed Gothic of north Oxford to the shallow pitched Italianate of Saltaire; Victorian houses come in all shapes, sizes and materials. At first glance, from the outside, they seem a confusing medley of historic styles and class aspirations, while inside, the lasting image is of a dark, cluttered, intimate atmosphere which wrapped the family in a protective cloak of randomly arranged pictures, richly coloured materials, small groupings of furniture around the fireplace and always, in a corner, the aspidistra!

For much of the 20th century, what can seem like cramped, fussy and often poorly arranged façades and interiors gave Victorian houses a bad reputation. Thanks, though, to the work of individuals like the late Poet Laureate, John Betjeman, and the charity The Victorian Society, attitudes towards 19th-century architecture have changed. In the past twenty years or so these spacious houses, with high ceilings, quality construction and the added charm of a hundred years or more of rustication, have become desirable once again.

For those millions of us, though, who live in a Victorian house or are interested in the subject, finding out about their history, who lived in them and what they originally looked like can be challenging. Architectural writers on the subject tend to be rather dismissive of this period of housing, with some justification. This book is intended, therefore, as an easy to understand guide, illustrated with my own drawings, diagrams and photographs, to help bridge this gap. It will provide readers with a fascinating background knowledge of all aspects of the Victorian house, whether they are renovating, tracing the history of their own house or simply want to know more about this notable period of history.

The book is divided into three sections. The first outlines the story of how houses developed through the period. Drawings and photos illustrate the different layouts, styles and dates when they were likely to have been built. Each chapter begins with a view from the small Staffordshire town of Leek, a 19th-century industrial centre whose growth mirrors that of towns throughout the rest of the country, but which unlike many others has retained most of its Victorian buildings. The second section steps inside and looks at the different rooms and their fittings, what they were used for and how they would have originally appeared. The final section is a quick reference guide with notes on dating houses, suggested books, places to visit and a glossary to explain some of the terms used.

Trevor Yorke

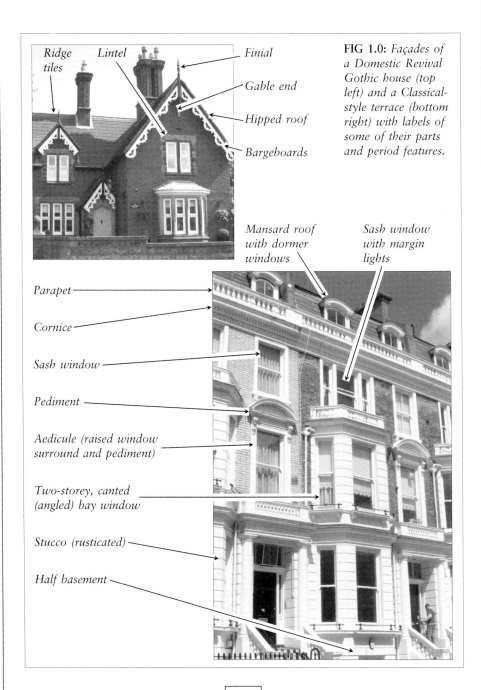

Ridge tiles

Lintel

Finial

Gable end

Hipped roof

Bargeboards

FIG 1.0: *Façades of a Domestic Revival Gothic house (top left) and a Classical-style terrace (bottom right) with labels of some of their parts and period features.*

Mansard roof with dormer windows

Sash window with margin lights

Parapet

Cornice

Sash window

Pediment

Aedicule (raised window surround and pediment)

Two-storey, canted (angled) bay window

Stucco (rusticated)

Half basement

SECTION I

THE HISTORY
OF THE
VICTORIAN
HOUSE

CHAPTER 1

The Background

FIG 1.1: *Saltaire, West Yorkshire: In 1853, Titus Salt did as many entrepreneurs of the day were doing and opened a new mill which incorporated numerous separate manufacturing processes for the first time under one roof (rear left of picture). Few, however, went on to build a complete village with sanitary housing, school, hospital, library and church for his employees, a rare benevolent action which took place over the 1850s and 1860s. The village was named after Titus 'Salt' and the River 'Aire' upon which it stood.*

The impression left by Victorian England is one of great contrasts. There is the perceived image of religious adherence and high family values, yet there was still child labour, poor public health and disease. We marvel at so many great inventions and impressive engineering projects, but forget the high loss of life in their creation and the intolerable working conditions of those who had to use them. We can still visit the gleaming steam engines and pristine country houses today, but without the filthy environment, smog and soot in which they originally stood. From this distance, the period appears a time of consistent financial success and international glory. However, this simple view masks the fluctuations, failures and depressions which struck at differing times throughout Victoria's long reign.

These same contrasts exist in their houses. Those which survive today are generally spacious and well built from good quality materials, with highly decorated façades. Yet the homes in which the majority of the working population lived were unhygienic, tiny and often poorly built, creating slums which have long since been flattened. Our image of Victorian buildings is therefore slightly skewed as so much of what was bad has been pulled down, while left standing are the quality structures or those with the space to permit adaptations for modern living.

When criticising modern housing, compared to the more decorative and better quality Victorian product, it is worth bearing in mind that a skilled worker who today might expect a three-bedroom semi with garden and all mod cons, in the 19th century would have sufficed with a two-bedroom terraced house and yard. Likewise, a small terrace house on the bottom of today's property ladder would have been a good-sized family home for a skilled factory worker in the 1850s.

The Victorian house has become popular again since the 1980s, especially compared with some of the

FIG 1.2: *Weavers' cottages in Holmsfirth, with the distinctive rows of windows illuminating the top workshop floors.*

plain and apparently flimsy housing on offer from the 1960s and 1970s. However, it should be noted that nearly three times more houses were erected in these decades than at the peak of Victorian building around 1900.

Although these points are aimed at removing our rose-tinted glasses before proceeding, this book is written not only as a hands-on practical guide to recognising and understanding Victorian houses but also as an enthusiastic celebration of these colourful, eccentric, eclectic and quality products of the industrial age. They were built to house a population which grew from eleven million in 1801 to thirty-two million a century later. Our story will begin with a look at where this bulging population lived.

Town and Village

Victorian England had a booming population, one that had been growing since the mid 18th century (principally due to a fall in the death rate of the very young) but which doubled between 1841 and 1901. At the same time, the number of people in each household dropped which, coupled with an expectation of more privacy and independence, led to greater demand for housing.

FIG 1.3: *Examples of Victorian semi-detached houses in North Oxford, with an Italianate style (top) and Gothic style (bottom), both dating from the 1860s and 1870s.*

The type and location of new building was to be greatly affected by the emergence of a new and increasingly influential social group – the middle class (although even by 1890 it accounted for less than 15% of the population). Those with a good education, a skilled job and a desire to demonstrate their success looked away from the cramped old Georgian terraces in the heart of the towns and cities. Instead, they were attracted to new developments on the edge of the urban area where the rapidly growing railway network still gave them easy access to the work place. These sub-urban estates, or suburbia, contained a variety of building types and sizes depending on whether they were aimed at lawyers, managers and doctors or clerks and tradesmen. The three commonest forms were the villa, the semi and the terraced house. Originally, villas were large detached estate houses in a landscaped setting but by the later 19th century the name could refer to almost any properties which were reasonably sized, detached or terraced and with a garden. Semis were not common yet and were often styled at this date to appear as a single detached house and hence raise their status. The bulk of suburban housing was terraced, usually one room wide and two deep, with a corridor running off from the front door, but as with all these housing types they became generally larger as the period went on, with more adaptations and extensions.

The growth of suburbia represented the new middle class's aspiration to appear respectable and at the same time to be separated from the lower classes.

In the towns and cities, the poor would no longer live alongside the educated professional. Instead, the ordinary workers moved to the old buildings in the centres of towns and cities that had been vacated by the middle classes. These buildings were often divided up and filled with a number of families so that the landlord could still achieve a reasonable income despite the lower individual rents.

New housing created for the poor was crammed into small plots and usually set around courtyards or along narrow, muddy back streets with, in the early years, no proper drainage or sanitation and only a communal water supply at best. The houses were either small terraces with through passages or back-to-backs, which were common in the industrial areas like Sheffield, Manchester, Leeds, Birmingham and Nottingham. These were terraced houses of one room depth which backed directly onto an identical row behind. They had no rear door and were surrounded on three of their four sides (figs 1.4 and 1.5). They were understandably unhygienic and, although as conditions improved local authorities forbade their construction, many were still being built in areas like Leeds right up to the end of the 19th century.

However, by 1900 conditions had improved and the poor working family who were likely to have lived in just one room when Victoria came to the throne could expect a small two-up two-down house by the time she passed on. A few fortunate workers might find themselves in the employment of a philanthropic

FIG 1.4: *A cut-away view of one type of back-to-back house, with a cellar for coal, a single living room and a bedroom above.*

FIG 1.5: *Restored back-to-backs in Inge Street, Birmingham (National Trust). Although they received a bad press in the 20th century, in their day they were a big improvement upon the single rooms working-class families had to share in many towns and cities (houses facing the street on the left and houses facing into the courtyard on the right).*

FIG 1.6: *Edensor, Derbyshire. When the 6th Duke of Devonshire decided Edensor rather spoilt the view from Chatsworth House, he had the village flattened and a series of individually designed, rather eccentric stone houses built out of sight in the late 1830s. Many of the designs in this model village were inspired by the influential* Encyclopedia of Cottage, Farm and Villa Architecture and Furniture *by J.C. Loudon.*

individual who, inspired either by religious benevolence or a desire to improve efficiency and create social stability, would build good quality housing for their staff. These new housing estates had proper sanitation, purpose-built churches, libraries and green spaces but rarely pubs! Famous examples include Saltaire, outside Leeds (fig 1.1), Port Sunlight on the Wirral and Bourneville to the south of Birmingham.

Despite the fluctuating drift of rural workers into the industrial towns and cities, the population of the countryside remained steady or even increased in the first half of the Victorian period. This was principally due to new settlements or extensions to existing ones being built to house workers for canals, railways, mining, quarrying, brickmaking and similar industries. Many villages in the later 18th and early 19th century became controlled environments, with any remaining common land enclosed and selected estate staff and tenant farmers tied to what was often the better quality housing. This process could also result in the eviction of casual agricultural labourers who could either try their luck in industry or struggle to find rural accommodation and end up in slum conditions worse than those in the cities. The modern image of the ideal English village, complete with a church, shop, school and rustic cottages set around a green, took shape in this period. There were few neat and trim rural settlements with these facilities before the 19th century.

The most notable aspect of rural housing from the late 18th century through to the second half of the 19th is the model villages erected by landowners to house their estate workers. Their motive for providing new accommodation was less likely to be benevolence than the improved efficiency of their estate or to make a more attractive backdrop through which guests could approach their country house. Sometimes villages were built on completely new sites, at other times on the flattened remains of former dwellings. As wealthy individuals funded such developments, professional architects were usually involved which has left us with a legacy of good quality, imaginative and sometimes eccentric buildings. These have often outlived the country house they were designed to complement!

Another type of building which architects could design in whimsical style was the gate-house. This stood singularly or in pairs at the entrance to the country house and was intended to give the guest a foretaste of the architectural wonders they were shortly to behold!

Farmhouses were often rebuilt in this period as landowners sought agricultural efficiency and tenant farmers better housing to match their aspirations now that they saw themselves as rural versions of the factory manager. As the last enclosure acts were passed in the first half of the Victorian period, particularly in the Midlands, the newly-grouped fields needed farms at their centre, not back in the villages where they had traditionally been, so stout red-brick or stone houses were erected in these isolated locations.

Victorian Estates

The majority of Victorian housing was in the form of either rows of streets or more luxurious landscaped developments on virgin fields. Such was the pressure to build on agricultural land that when its value for farming became less than the money which could be made from the approaching wave of suburban housing the landowner sought to convert it. He could either sell or lease the land to an individual or estate development company, or it could be divided up and sold block by block to speculative builders. In some cases the original landlord retained the land and developed the estate himself.

The layout of the streets on the new developments could be affected by what went before as it was usual for the existing country lanes and roads to be retained in the new pattern. Even today, in our towns and cities, these old routes can be identified by looking back at maps which pre-date the development. Although at the top end of the housing market streets may have been set out with tree-lined pavements and services laid on to the properties, in the poorer examples there was no proper planning and many had just narrow lanes in front of their houses. Acts of Parliament and local bye-laws enforced the provision of drainage, water supply and stipulated road widths. However, this only gradually improved the situation for many in the second half of the century.

A useful way to date a development and hence the houses is from the street name. Many were named after events or people, which can be pinpointed in some cases to a precise date. Some like Inkerman (fig 1.7), Sebastapol, Balaclava and Alma were named after battles in the Crimean War of 1853-6. Others commemorated an event, like Beaconsfield Street after the Prime Minister Disraeli became earl of that town. Some celebrated royalty – Hanover Street recognised the country's German connections in the first part of the 19th century, for instance, while Coronation Street could simply be dated to around the years 1838 and 1902 (the coronations being in the year after the death of the previous monarch). Some names may not help with dating but can record an aspect of the history of the site, perhaps the name of the last aristocratic owner, the manor in which it was sited, or a long lost feature.

Speculative Builders

Although there were a number of different ways in which the landowner could set about developing his site, the most common situation, once the plans for the new estate and its streets had been laid out, was for the land to be divided up into separate plots. In the 19th century there were few large building companies and most of our terraces were erected by speculative builders. Due to limited funds they would buy up a small number of plots and build just a short row of houses. Although a street of terraced houses today may look as if it was built by the same hand at one time, closer observation of the joints between houses and subtle differences in their styling can show where one builder finished and another started (fig 1.8).

FIG 1.7: *Documentary evidence confirms that this row was built in 1855 in the aftermath of the Battle of Inkerman. Although initially celebrated, stories later emerged which discredited the victory and after a few years it was quietly forgotten, so any road named thus will probably date from this narrow period.*

FIG 1.8: *On closer inspection of a row of terraced houses you can usually find joints where the bricks do not line up, indicating that one side was built at a later date or by a different builder.*

This piecemeal development of estates was partly due to the limited resources of these small builders. They often started out as joiners or bricklayers and could only borrow or scrape together enough money to build a few houses. Despite the boom in housing profit, margins were tight, limited by the fact that nearly everyone rented property rather than buying it. Even by the end of the 19th century, fewer than 10% of householders owned their house. Small builders had the choice of being commissioned to build and receiving a payment upon completion, selling their speculative development on to a landlord, or renting out the properties directly, therefore only receiving a gradual repayment for their outlay over time.

Because of these tight margins and the risk of falling into debt, speculative builders tended to play safe with the style and design of houses. They chose well-established forms and proven popular fashions. Unfortunately, this often meant that they simply ordered period features from catalogues and slapped them onto regular-sized structures of inappropriate proportions, with little understanding of the style they sought to imitate. This is the main reason why the professional architects of the time (and many commentators today) tend to dismiss the bulk of this housing as amateurish, watered-down versions of their own work for the upper classes. To the speculative builder, though, these hotchpotches of colourful brickwork patterns and elaborately-styled details attracted prospective tenants through the general aura and social status implied by the style of the house rather than by its architectural perfection.

It is fair to say that at the bottom end of the market, i.e. the mass housing for the poor where profits were very tight, corners were cut and bad reputations justified. The term 'jerry-building' appears at this time, coming from the sea-faring name for temporary repairs to sails and rigging known as 'jury-rig'. It described poor quality houses put up too quickly, with too few materials and which, in the main, have long since been demolished.

Methods and Materials

Until the coming of the industrial age and its acceleration with the spread of the railways, most housing was broadly termed as vernacular, that is, it was constructed by local builders using local materials. They passed down the traditional methods of that region from master to apprentice and due to the difficulty and cost of transport they tended to make the most of resources in the area. The exceptions were the houses of the aristocracy who could afford to bring in better materials and professional architects to design buildings in styles reminiscent of distant lands, in what is termed Polite Architecture.

The process of change began in the late 18th century and rapidly spread in the 19th as builders had a wider choice of cheaper materials from further away and could use published plans which met the demands of a more stylistically aware clientele. Ordering materials and keeping a tight rein on the costs was easier as bricks became more regular in size, stone was available to precise measurements from catalogues and house plans were standardised. Houses were no longer individual extensions of the local geology, but became regular rows of foreign forms overwhelming the landscape. Despite this, some local variation in materials still existed through into the 20th century; stone, for instance, was still popular in the regions where it was extracted and bricks were produced in numerous small works with their colour affected by the local clay and methods of firing.

Walls

The well-built Victorian house would usually have its foundations dug down through the top soil until a firm footing

FIG 1.9: *A brick (top) and a stone house (bottom) showing how the best quality material was used on the front (left) but cheaper was permissible down the sides (right).*

was found and then a flared or stepped base to the wall was built to carry the weight above. Next up would be the damp course, a perpetual problem with numerous solutions of varying success, mainly from the 1850s. A common arrangement was to have a timber ground floor suspended with ventilation grilles in the wall to keep air circulating beneath. A layer of impervious material like slate, asphalt and tar, lead or zinc sheeting would be inserted into the wall just below it. Later on, a couple of courses of dark grey/blue engineering bricks were found to be a more effective barrier. When there was a basement room the outer surfaces of its walls were typically coated with asphalt to keep water out although this was unlikely to be done in an unoccupied cellar or underground storage.

The walls above were usually solid in this period although in some regions cavity walls with an inner and outer skin of brick and a gap between can be found with either bricks, metal ties or the surrounds of doors and windows holding the two sides together. The thickness of solid brick walls is usually around nine inches. This was determined by the length of a single brick which, depending on the pattern by which it was laid (the bonding), would at some point go across from front to back to give strength to the structure (see fig 1.11). Different bonds were formed from stretchers, bricks laid with the long side showing, and headers with the short end exposed. The various patterns formed were popular at different times. In the first half of the period, the most widely used was

Flemish bond. This found popularity particularly in the Midlands and South while later English bond, which was regarded as stronger and more in keeping with the Revival styles of the time, gained favour and is often found in the North. Both of these styles had cheaper variants which put a number of courses of stretchers between each row of the pattern to keep costs down. It was also acceptable for a good quality brick, laid in an expensive form with fine joints, to be used for the public face of a house, with cheaper bricks used on the side, dividing and back walls (see fig 1.9).

The walls were still held together in this period by lime mortar cement until, in the last decades of the century, harder Portland cements became popular. Lime mortar was made from crushed limestone or chalk, which was heated in a kiln to produce quicklime (calcium oxide), then mixed with water to create lime putty (calcium hydroxide). It had to be left for months in storage before use. It was then mixed with sand or similar aggregates to make the final mortar cement, although it could be used neat to produce fine joints. In some industrial areas, dark materials like ash, iron fillings or the black sand used in metal mouldings were mixed into the mortar to blacken it, pre-empting the colour it would become in the sooty atmosphere! In areas of the South and East, galleting was sometimes used, when small pebbles or flints were inserted into the mortar joint before it set.

The finished mortar joint was usually flush with the brickwork or slightly recessed. A unique form of joint which can still be found in the high-class work of this period was tuck pointing which created an apparently precise narrow joint. The mortar was removed back a short way and a special pointing mortar which had been coloured with brick dust to match the wall was inserted and brought up flush with the surface. Then a fine groove was cut into it as it dried and neat lime putty inserted with the aid of a rule to complete the illusion of a fine joint.

Lime mortar cement can take years to fully harden, it is susceptible to the elements and, more importantly, it is porous. This creates a problem when a wall is repointed with modern impervious cements as they force any moisture out through the bricks rather

FIG 1.10: *Examples of brickwork with locally-produced bricks laid in Flemish bond (above) and later fine jointed machine-cut Accrington reds laid in English bond (below).*

than the joints, causing the bricks to flake away.

Bricks

Although our image of Victorian England is of large factories belching smoke, most industry in the 19th century actually took place on numerous small sites. This was very much the case in brickmaking, where there were more than 1,500 brickworks, each employing an average of between ten to fifteen men. The increase in output which made brick so affordable came from improvements in traditional methods as well as from mechanisation, such as machines for grinding clay and filling moulds and new kilns for firing. A rise in demand also occurred after 1850, with new fashions for exposed brickwork and the repeal of the Brick Tax. This had

been levied on the quantity used in a building for the past seventy years and encouraged the production of larger size bricks and rat bonding (standing the bricks up so their bases face out to reduce the total number used). With its passing, machine-made bricks of a precise, standard size were produced with sharp edges so they could be laid with thin joints between them.

Previously, brickworks had been sited locally. With the spread of the railways they could now move to where the clays they needed were being dug out of the ground and there was a good source of fuel to help reduce production costs. This led to the growth of brickworks in selected parts of England, each with a distinctive product which could now be transported across the country. These included the Accrington reds from Lancashire, which were branded

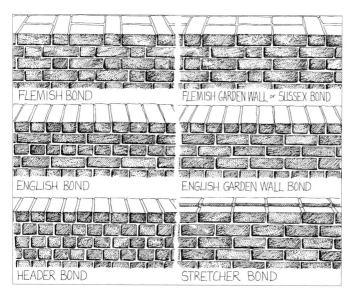

FIG 1.11:
Drawings of the different types of brick bonding which were common in the Victorian period. The arrangement through the wall is exposed at the top of each example.

'Nori', iron spelt backwards, as they were very dense, smooth and sharp edged. Staffordshire blues or engineering bricks were made from a clay with a high iron content and fired at up to 1,200 degrees Celsius, making an impervious blue/grey brick, ideal for damp courses. New machines for extraction appeared in the late 19th century, making it possible to reach the Oxford clays around Bedfordshire. This led to the industrial scale production of Fletton bricks which were cheap because less work was required in preparing and firing the raw material, although in the Victorian period they were mainly used for dividing and interior walls. At the same time, local types were still popular in their home regions, for instance the white bricks made from clays in chalk beds which were especially popular around Cambridge, silver-grey brick around Reading from the use of wood in the firing, and yellow bricks due to the slow firing of magnesium and iron rich clay in the London area.

Stone

Certain areas of England, where stone is close at hand, have traditionally used it for housing and despite the overwhelming popularity of brick this continued, especially as steam-powered machines aided extraction and the railways improved transportation, thus making it cheaper. Millstone grit was used for back-to-backs in the mill towns of Yorkshire and Lancashire, slate and granite were the backbone of fashionable Victorian houses and hotels in the Lake District, while limestone was still used across its traditional zone from Dorset through to the Wash.

Stone walls could be constructed in a number of ways. In higher-class buildings or those made from certain stones like millstone grit, which could be easily cut, the wall could be made like brick with squared off blocks and a smooth finished surface (ashlar). The joints between stones were often opened out with chamfers or mouldings, usually on the bottom floor of more prestigious housing (rustication), with a smooth or patterned surface (the latter was often simulated in stucco, see p31). With harder rocks and on cheaper houses, stones had minimal shaping and were stacked depending on their regularity in either vague courses or

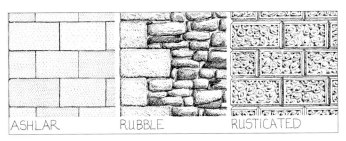

FIG 1.12:
Examples of three different ways in which stone walls could be laid and finished.

ASHLAR   RUBBLE   RUSTICATED

completely at random (rubble), although the corners still had solid blocks to make the quoins. Facing stones could also be used on top of a brick or rubble core.

The most common use of stone in this period was for lintels (the solid bar above a window or door), sills (the solid piece beneath) and for decorative mouldings. The stone could be cut to standard sizes in the quarry, then transported to anywhere in the country at cheap enough prices for it to be used even in the mass terraced housing for the working classes. By the late 19th century, labour costs and difficulties with the supply of some stone helped to make alternative materials, like terracotta, a popular choice for decorative pieces on houses, and brick lintels became fashionable again.

Glass

Glass was another aspect of the Victorian house to be affected by new technology. Previously, windows had usually been fitted with crown glass, which was made by blowing and spinning the molten glass to form a disc. This was then cut down into individual panes. This method only produced small pieces, which can still be recognised today from bubbles within the glass. By 1840, new methods of producing plate glass, which was poured onto a table and hand polished, and cylinder glass, where large sheets were cut from a molten cylinder of glass, both produced much bigger window panes. Therefore, the standard sash window in the mid-

Victorian period had four panes and by the later 19th century just two. One problem with these large panes of glass was that without the glazing bars the structure of the sliding sashes was weakened. Windows in the early Victorian period, like their Regency predecessors, had evolved very thin glazing bars. As larger sheets of glass became available, the wooden frames became thicker, with the top sash having little horns projecting down on its underside to enable a stronger mortice and tenon joint to be formed in its corners (see fig 1.13).

FIG 1.13: *A Victorian sash window. Note that the box which held the counterweights and pulleys was recessed behind the brick wall, a regulation which was only relaxed in 1894.*

FIG 1.14: *Examples, from top to bottom, of a sash, casement and a cross window (vertical mullions and horizontal transom).*

In the first half of the 19th century, a window tax and excise duty on glass were still imposed so builders were restrained in their fitting, although the presence of a bricked up aperture may not mean a window has been blocked up to avoid paying. It might have been built to keep the symmetry of a façade without limiting the use of the wall on the inside. When the taxes were abolished in the 1850s builders reintroduced the previously expensive bay window, which found its way onto even the most humble of houses by the end of the century.

Although the sash window dominated, other types were used. The horizontal or Yorkshire sash did not require pulleys and weights as it moved left to right and hence was cheaper. It was often used on working class housing, especially in the limited space under the eaves. Hinged opening casement windows, fixed mullions with leaded lights, dormer and oriel windows were all traditional types of window popular in the 16th and 17th century which were reintroduced with the Revival styles of the Victorian period. These different types will be discussed in more detail along with changing styles of sash windows in the following chapters.

Roofs

Slate dramatically changed the design of roofs in the 19th century, especially Welsh slate which became widely available and cheap due to improved methods of extraction and transport. Its ease of use made it popular with speculative builders as it was supplied in standard sizes, usually around 2 ft by 1 ft. It could simply be nailed to battens which ran horizontally across the rafters and it only needed replacing every 100 years or so. Its light weight also meant that the pitch of the roof could be lowered, which was convenient when trying to hide it behind a parapet (see fig 1.16) as was the fashion in the first half of the century.

There were other slates, like the green and blue tinged ones from the Lake District and the dark greys from Cornwall and South Wales. Other stones which could easily be broken into flat slabs and were still referred to as slates included limestone in the Cotswolds and millstone grits in Yorkshire and Lancashire. These heavier pieces were supplied to site in a variety of sizes and tended to need steeper pitched roofs to take the weight. They also had to be sorted into size with the smaller ones at the top and the largest pieces at the bottom above the eaves. This was probably so that the area where the most rainwater collected near the eaves was covered by the largest pieces, which also had their weight on the strongest point above the walls (see fig 1.15).

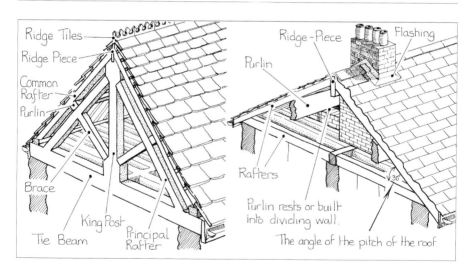

FIG 1.15: *Views of roofs with their internal trusses exposed. The left-hand view shows a type which could be found in a better class of house with a steeper pitched roof to take the weight of the stone tiles (note the sizes from small at the top to large at the bottom).The right shows an arrangement which was common in standard terraced housing, in this case with a low pitched slate roof dating from the first half of the 19th century.*

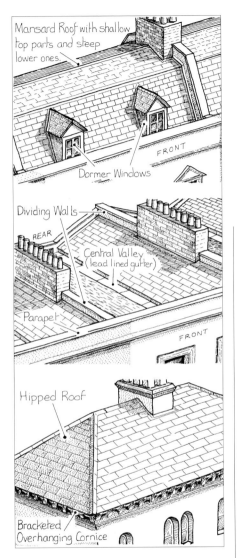

Mansard Roof with shallow top parts and steep lower ones.

Dormer Windows

FRONT

Dividing Walls

REAR

Central Valley (lead lined gutter)

Parapet

FRONT

Hipped Roof

Bracketed / Overhanging Cornice

FIG 1.16: *Three examples of roof types. The mansard roof with a steep and shallow pitch combined was a clever way of creating more height in the attic. The middle view shows an arrangement popular in Classical terraces with a parapet hiding a slate roof with a central valley draining off at the rear (always a weak point for leaks). The last view is of a hipped roof, popular on some Italianate and later Arts and Crafts houses.*

windows and cupolas (small doomed features fitted to the ridge of roofs), lead was still used despite its expense. It was produced by pouring the molten lead onto a bed covered with damp sand, to be quickly spread and smoothed before hardening, though from the 1830s sets of rollers produced a more consistent thickness (milled lead).

From the 1850s fashion brought the roof out from behind the parapet and made a feature of it, while the variety of materials available increased with the introduction of machine-made roofing tiles in the 1870s. Numerous types of tiles had always been used, like pantiles which were characteristic in the East of England. However, with mass production a wider choice of small, machine-made coloured tiles proved popular as they were considered more interesting and appropriate for Revival houses than the often monotonous slate.

For the most shallow roofs, or those with tricky arrangements as on dormer

CHAPTER 2

Later Regency and Early Victorian
1830–1850

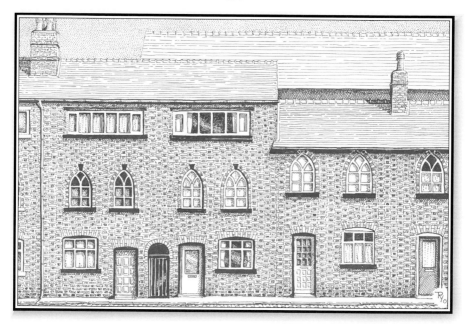

FIG 2.1: *Weavers' cottages in London Street, Leek, dating from the 1820s and 1830s.*

When Queen Victoria ascended the throne in 1837, the small market town of Leek on the south western edge of the Peak District was in the process of industrial expansion, principally around the production of silk. At this date, though, there were only a handful of mills. Much of the work was still domestic, typically in cottages with elongated rows of small windows, south or west facing to illuminate the workshops which ran over a number of homes (see fig 2.1). The remainder of the workforce lived in modest two-up two-downs or tiny houses set around courts at the rear of larger premises. Disease was prevalent, mainly due to

FIG 2.2: *This early Victorian house would have been at the top end of working-class accommodation in its day. It has multi-pane sash windows (with no horns), plain stone lintels, Flemish bond brickwork and a flat pitched roof, all characteristic of the period.*

1824, the Leek Building Society formed with forty-two shares to be paid for at one guinea a month for six years, entitling the subscriber to a new house. By 1832 these houses had all been built on the edge of town, after which the society was wound up (hence 'Terminating'). The gas works, built in 1827, supplied lighting but this was mainly used by factories and the new street lights, which were paid for by the commissioners. However, their use was limited to autumn and winter, with only half lit at any one time and none at all around the nights of a full moon!

For the more successful and better off, new houses were erected along the eastern edge of Leek, although some still chose to live in the smarter streets in town despite their close proximity to the workers' slums. The booming population also prompted the creation of a new parish for the eastern end of town, St Luke's church in a new Gothic revival style being completed in 1848 and its associated vicarage, a smart detached stone house, following ten years later.

the poor drainage, with privies emptying out into cesspools through open gutters where people worked. Water supply for most was from springs or wells while those fortunate enough to have a piped source found it unreliable and from a reservoir which was reported to be infested with fish and frogs.

Improvement Commissioners and a Board of Health were appointed but, with little legislation in place, their efforts were limited. The formation of Terminating Building Societies helped workers to invest in better housing. In

THE NATIONAL PICTURE

The development of this small Staffordshire town was being mirrored across most of the urban areas of England in the first half of the 19th century. There were no clear class divides or social identities. It was still possible to find workers residing in the same neighbourhoods as the rich. Wages and conditions could be just as diverse, depending on the area or industry the individual worked in. There was a large overlap in earnings between skilled workers and educated clerks. The same

FIG 2.3: *Bow windows were popular in the Regency and early Victorian period, like this example from Oxford which still retains the casings for the exterior blinds at the top of the first floor windows. Deep overhanging, shallow pitched roofs were also a feature of houses in the first half of the 19th century.*

diversity existed in the country where agricultural labourers might earn up to twice as much in areas like Lancashire, where their employers had to compete with the more attractive jobs in the mills, than in more remote rural districts. For most workers in this period, though, housing was poor with an average family expected to live in only one or two rooms, be it in a new house or an older one divided up. Multiple occupation was common with an average of around ten people per house when Victoria ascended

the throne. These cramped conditions in turn created health problems. Epidemics were frequent and restricted life expectancy to an average of 40 years in 1839, while for some in the worst urban slums it was only fifteen.

In this period, those in polite society who had found urban life fashionable were now looking for houses away from the filth, disease and factories of the old centres, and moving to more exclusive and private estates. The increasing number of educated, white collar workers sought to mirror their social superiors. For the first time, with the rapid expansion of the railway in the 1840s, people were able to commute from their new suburban terraces into town. By 1850, around 6,000 miles of track had been laid. This also brought increasing numbers of holidaymakers to the expanding coastal resorts, where large, painted, terraced houses with rows of expansive bow windows were lining the seafronts. The pressure of urban growth and the success of non-conformist groups in these areas was such that a re-invigorated Church of England began to respond by creating new parishes, churches and, hence, vicarages in towns and cities to serve the shifting population.

Many new workers came from the countryside directly surrounding a town, attracted by better pay, conditions, freedom and fun. The work in factories, however hard to our modern eyes, was probably less strenuous than agricultural labour. It had become increasingly difficult to live in many villages as the last phase of enclosures had enabled major landowners to snap up the common land and keep a tight rein on the occupants of their cottages. Casual agricultural workers either had to put up with appalling housing or move to the urban areas. Unfortunately, these migrants from the country also brought livestock with them. The yards of their tiny houses, which were crammed around courts or along streets, were infested with animals, another rich area for the spread of disease.

THE STRUCTURE OF HOUSES
Large and Medium Houses

The houses built for the aristocrats, industrialists, businessmen or professionals in this period could take a number of forms: the villa, the semi and, by far the most popular option, the terraced house. The builder of a detached property had a much wider scope for structural design than for those built in a row, and the style chosen could have a direct effect upon its plan. Classical villas had appeared in the late 18th and early 19th century, emulating the fashionable country houses in a more compact urban form while retaining the symmetry and correct proportions in their façades. Alongside these were houses which ignored the tight Classical reins and had an asymmetrical plan which permitted more freedom with the arrangement of rooms. Now armed with influential books like John Loudon's *Encyclopedia of Cottage, Farm and Villa Architecture and Furniture*, packed with designs for houses, even speculative builders could embark upon these ambitious plans.

The terraced houses built for this affluent group were larger than their Georgian predecessors. The extra space was created by adding more storeys (four, five or even six levels, including a basement and attic, were becoming common) and by extending to the rear (the width of the plots remained similar). The basement was often raised up so that only half of it was

FIG 2.4: *A selection of houses from Edensor, Derbyshire (see fig 1.6) which were built in the late 1830s and early 1840s with no house the same as another. The buildings in this model village were inspired by examples from J.C. Loudon's* Encyclopedia of Cottage, Farm and Villa Architecture and Furniture *(first edition published c.1833).*

underground (a half basement), which reduced the amount the builder had to excavate and made the approach to the front door, which was now up steps, more dramatic. Ceiling heights, especially in the principal rooms, were also increasing by about a foot while the front rooms could benefit from a bow or bay window. This was especially popular in seaside resorts where it commanded a better view of the scenery and the people promenading by. There was also a fashion for letting the greenery outside reflect within so doors were opened between front and rear rooms, mirrors carefully positioned

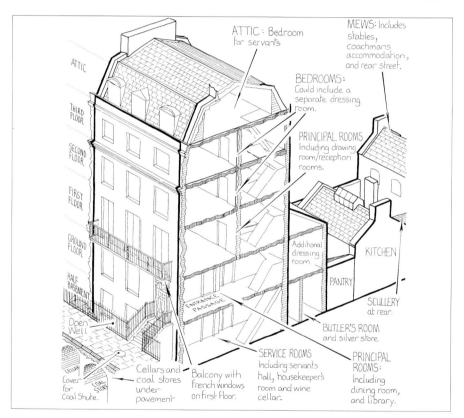

FIG 2.5: *A cut-away view showing the structural elements of a large early Victorian terraced house. The medium-sized version for the better paid professional would emulate many of these features, only usually with three to four storeys (including a basement), on a narrower plot of land and probably with just a simple rear extension.*

and French windows fitted to open out onto first-floor balconies.

In the largest houses, where more accommodation was required for servants and the increasingly specialised service rooms, extensions to the rear became common, enabling the noisy, smelly and potentially inflammable kitchen to be moved from the basement and a servants' hall, housekeeper's rooms, and cellars to take their place. The arrival of piped water which could be supplied at improved but different pressures created a new room in this class of house – the scullery – which was usually sited next to the kitchen. Unfortunately, the drains which ran along the backs were still limited and without traps were prone to emitting a foul stench. These simple rear extensions meant the main structure of the house could remain two rooms deep, therefore avoiding stretching the already tricky

roof arrangement. For both the large terraced or detached house, the mews at the rear or in a nearby street was the 19th-century version of a garage, where horses, carriages and stable hands were accommodated.

The increase in levels permitted extra bedrooms now that boys and girls from this class were expected to sleep in separate rooms, while the attic above was usually for the servants' sleeping quarters. There would not usually be a bathroom at this date, and only a few might have running hot water, though the small extra rooms created by the rear extension could accommodate a dressing room or closet.

There was also a small number of semi-detached houses, usually with the main body similar in form to a terraced house, with two floors and an attic above and a half basement below. The main difference with the extra width of the plot was a low extension to the side, which accommodated the main door.

Medium and Small Houses

The new houses built for the growing population of white-collar staff and industrial workers could range in size from three-storey buildings with a cellar, down to small back-to-backs. As much industry at this date was still domestic, houses with a third open floor above the bedrooms providing a workshop were still being built (fig 2.1). Two-up two-downs with a cellar or yard containing coal storage and ash bins were at the top end of working class accommodation (fig 2.2). A variety of plans existed, designed to cram as many houses into small plots

FIG 2.6: *Early Victorian semis with the front doors in a lower extension linking the houses.*

as possible, with up to 100 houses per acre recorded and certain layouts and types popular in specific locations. Common to all the designs, assuming that they were to be used by one family, were one or two living rooms on the ground floor, one of which would have been used for cooking, with one or two bedrooms on the floor above. A cast-iron range and running water were unlikely to be found at this date.

Roofs were typically low-pitched and covered in slate. Walls were generally plain, often still with brick-arched lintels above the windows and doors. The single

piece stone lintels were not readily available yet, away from the areas where they were produced. Featureless chimneys cluttered the skyline and rainwater barrels, coal sheds and communal privies the congested yards and narrow lanes below.

It is hard to associate one size or style of house with a particular type of worker in the first half of the 19th century. Wages could vary dramatically across the country for the same job as there were no unions or workers' rights to enforce a national salary scale. However, the cost of building a house was more even throughout England, due to improved transport making cheaper materials available. It was the local economy and the wages that companies had to pay to get staff in that area which would determine who rented what size of house. It is also worth noting that due to their poor quality and squalid sites, very little of the above housing has survived into the 21st century, with only the better two-up two-downs for the factory supervisor or local shopkeeper, or exceptional cases of model houses likely to be found.

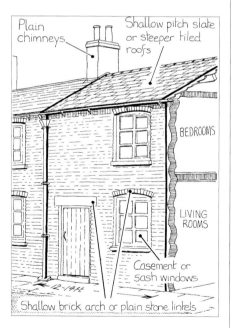

FIG 2.7: *A drawing of a basic two-up two-down, highlighting some of the features which were common in this period.*

THE STYLE OF HOUSES

During the first half of the 19th century, academics, gentlemen and religious theologians argued for and against appropriate styles for the nation's buildings. The sides were drawn out principally between the Classical, whose tight rules of order had dominated polite architecture for the past two centuries and the more recent Gothic revival, which had emerged out of misty views of picturesque scenery and romantic tales of England's medieval past. Although the bulk of housing in this period was either too poor for decoration to be an issue or only good enough to permit a few token applied details, there was an increasing number of large terraces and detached houses where the emerging specialist professional, the architect, could explore new forms from these historic or foreign sources.

Classical

Classical architecture is a return to the artistic rules of ancient Rome and later Greece. It probably first arrived in this country sometime in the early 16th century (after the Renaissance rebirth of Classicism on the continent) although it was not until the 17th century that it began to dominate English domestic architecture. The interpretation of its principals of form, proportion and style fluctuated in severity through the generations. During the Regency and early Victorian period there was a rejection of the former strict and logical Neo-Classical style, in favour of more flamboyant and picturesque forms.

Regency and early Victorian Classical houses are distinctive in a number of ways from their fine but plain brick and stone Georgian predecessors. The most notable difference is the use of stucco, a smooth, painted rendering. It was less expensive than the real stone it sought to imitate and masked the use of cheap bricks and materials. Stucco was used either just on the ground floor levels to save costs, to highlight doors and windows and form decorative

FIG 2.8: *Belgrave Square, London. This square with communal gardens in the centre was built by Thomas Cubitt, the most successful speculative builder of his time. In exclusive rows of Regency and early Victorian terraces like these, the central and end blocks were often emphasised with giant columns and pediments, giving the whole row the effect of being a single Classical country house. This fashion died out in the 1840s.*

columns, cornices and brackets, or it could completely cover the façade in its protective coat (a property which made it very popular at seaside resorts). It was formed by building up two or three coats of render (which by this period were likely to be cements) over rows of battens, which could be removed at the end, and finished to form the distinctive grooves which were popular on the lower storeys to emulate the rusticated masonry bases of larger Classical buildings. It was painted the colour of stone, usually a local one, although

Bath stone was universally copied. Some could even be enhanced by weathering effects achieved using amongst other things milk and blood!

In the Regency period, sash windows were divided up by fine glazing bars, typically into twelve panes. However, by the early Victorian period, the increasing availability of larger sheets of glass saw the introduction of the four-pane window. The rectangular surround (sometimes square on the top floor) still tended to be plain although by this time there was a move to emphasise the individual features of a façade and simple mouldings began to

appear around windows. Six-panelled front doors were popular in the first half of the century but by the late 1840s the standard Victorian four-panelled door was dominant. On good quality houses they were made from a hardwood, occasionally from the 1830s with glass in the upper panels, while cheaper houses used poorer woods which were either painted to simulate an expensive wood like oak, or just finished in a plain colour. Square-headed classical doorcases formed out of stucco or stone, some with a porch supported on columns or forming part of the balcony above, were common on the better class of house. Other houses may have been plain as cheap wood doorcases were not permitted under fire regulations.

It was still usual to have a fanlight above the door to illuminate the passage beyond. An arched shape or rectangle with a semicircle set within it was popular in the Regency, with plain glass fanlights appearing from the 1830s. Before 1840, mail had to be paid for by the recipient. However, with the introduction of the penny post, with stamps bought by the sender, there was no need for anyone to answer the door, so letterboxes began to appear. At first they were clumsily fitted into existing doors until new doors with a wider central bar (muntin) were introduced after this date.

Balconies, usually on the first floor from which the well-to-do could watch the world pass by, were a common early 19th-century feature. Many were enclosed by elaborate ironwork railings, sometimes with lead or copper-covered canopies above and usually painted in an

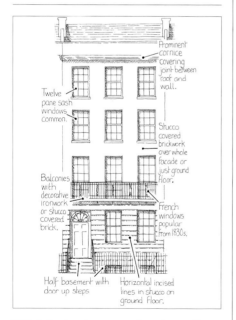

Twelve pane sash windows common.

Prominent cornice covering joint between roof and wall.

Stucco covered brickwork over whole facade or just ground floor.

Balconies with decorative ironwork or stucco covered brick.

French windows popular from 1830s.

Half basement with door up steps.

Horizontal incised lines in stucco on ground floor.

FIG 2.9: *An elevation of a Classically-styled large terraced house, highlighting some of the typical features from this period.*

antique green or bronze effect. Others had stone or stucco balustrades to match the rest of the house. At the top of the better class façade there would have been a parapet, now with a pronounced cornice running horizontally just below it, a convenient feature which helped cover up the joint between the wall and the shallow-pitched roof behind. In the more modest Classically-styled terrace, the upper walls may have been exposed brick, sometimes with just a simple parapet following the contours of the V-shaped roof line which was still common in this period.

Gothic

Gothic architecture is based upon the pointed arch, its name being an insult coined by Classical architectural commentators who compared it to the barbarian Goths, against their superior Roman style. The revival of this medieval form began in the 18th century, firstly on whimsical minor estate buildings and follies and then, after Strawberry Hill (Horace Walpole's Twickenham house, built during the 1750-70s), as a fashionable style for the main house. This earlier form is referred to as Gothick with a 'k' to differentiate it from the more historically accurate forms of the Victorian period, and stuccoed houses in this style still appeared in the early 19th century. Its distinctive features include pointed windows, which tend to be squat with wide arches and intersecting Y-shaped window bars (see fig 2.1), hood mouldings above the larger rectangular windows and pointed gables, some with stepped battlements. If the exterior was

not completely covered in stucco, the decorative details and window surrounds were often still formed out of it. However, the general form of the house was very similar to the Classical, with builders using familiar forms and just applying the Gothick detailing.

Alongside these were 'Olde English' style cottages which developed from a growing appreciation for the picturesque and an emerging desire for the quaint and reassuring traditional forms in the wake of the Industrial Revolution. These are often found in the new planned villages of the first half of the 19th century, as individual buildings in older settlements or around a country estate. When they are found in towns they could be associated with a large mansion, which has been later surrounded or swallowed up by urban developments. The distinctive features of these cottages are steeper-pitched tiled or thatched roofs, Tudor-style chimneys and elaborately carved bargeboards on the pointed gables.

During the 1820s and 1830s, for the first time, there were accurate archaeological studies of medieval structures, a wide availability of Gothic antiques from Northern Europe after the French Revolution and Napoleonic Wars (1793-1815) and a growing number of publications detailing and extolling the virtues of true Gothic architecture. Its greatest exponent was A. W. N. Pugin who, following his conversion to the newly enfranchised Catholic Church (after the Catholic Emancipation Act of 1829), produced influential books outlining his principles of 'Pointed or Christian Architecture'. He believed that buildings should be honest in laying bare their materials, construction and function and deplored the sham, stucco-covered façades which were still in fashion. Decoration of surfaces should be two-dimensional, patterned brickwork rather than applied detail raised above the surface of the wall, as was often formed out of stucco on Classical houses of the time. He also advocated asymmetrical planning which freed the designer to lay out the rooms to a more appropriate size and position for their function, without the restrictions of trying to make them fit behind a symmetrical Classical façade. The true impact of Pugin was to influence the next generation of architects. In this period, much of his own time was spent on the rebuilding of the Houses of Parliament and designing new Catholic churches,

now they were free to openly pray. He did produce a number of large houses but one of the few places you might find early examples of this pure form of Gothic is on the houses built for the clergy, where this true medieval style was immediately appreciated. Features of this style are steep pitched, plain grey slate roofs, the use of red-brick with stone mouldings around pointed arched or square-headed traceried windows and doorways, Gothic porches and projecting oriel windows.

Historic and Exotic

The Napoleonic Wars heightened a nationalistic passion for England's glorious past and encouraged many of the aristocracy to raise sham castles and 'Elizabethan' mansions, with elements of these historic styles filtering down to

FIG 2.10 (left): A late Regency/early Victorian villa with a low pitched hipped roof, twelve and sixteen-pane sash windows and a semi-circular fanlight.

FIG 2.11 (right): *The rear of a row of terraces in London. Like many in this period they still had a low pitched roof with a central valley, the rain water draining out through a gutter at the rear. This 'V' shape may have been hidden behind a parapet at the front.*

more modest structures, often for estate housing to complement the main building. Discoveries in Egypt brought a short-lived fashion in the Regency for this ancient style, although usually in decoration rather than external form. The same was true of exotic styles inspired by China and India, which became popular after the expansion of trade with the Far East in the early 19th century. All these forms were generally whimsical detached oddities and stylised decoration, and although only the so-called Elizabethan style continued into

FIG 2.13: *Semi-circular fanlights were still popular into the early Victorian period, before the rectangular shape became dominant.*

FIG 2.12: *Two houses from a Classically-styled Victorian terrace. Period details include the French windows opening out onto a balcony with iron railings and the use of twelve-pane sash windows. This example also features raised mouldings around the windows, pediments above the openings on the first floor (piano noble) and a deep cornice over the second floor, details which became popular in the 1840s and 1850s. The house is stuccoed and on the ground floor it has horizontal incised lines to imitate a similar effect on stone buildings.*

FIG 2.14: *An early Gothic building with mock 14th and 15th-century details like the deep hood moulds above the windows and doors and the steep pointed arch on the fanlight.*

the Victorian period, the acceptability of a variety of styles from different sources is one of the main features of 19th-century housing.

FIG 2.16 (above): *Locally produced brick laid in Flemish bond and typical of the first half of the 19th century.*

FIG 2.18 (below): *A smaller middle-class terrace (compared with fig 2.12) with stucco limited to the lower floors and only used around the windows above to save cost. It still has its balcony, French windows and blind casings.*

FIG 2.15: *Bow windows were a popular feature on Regency and early Victorian houses.*

FIG 2.17 (left): *A typical sash window from the early 19th century with twelve panes, its frame recessed behind the exterior brickwork and no horns in the bottom corners of the top sash.*

CHAPTER 3

Mid Victorian Houses 1850–1870

FIG 3.1: *Wellington Mill, Leek: New, larger factories and mills like this one dating from 1853 began to dominate the skyline of Leek and other industrial towns as numerous processes were now combined under one roof. Around these factories new terraces were built, generally larger, some with their own yards and even decoration with the use of coloured bricks.*

L eek continued to grow during these two mid-Victorian decades as new, larger mills towered over the expanding suburban terraces. Workshops were rarely built in the terraces as by 1870 domestic weaving had almost died out. Down in the surrounding river valley, dye works were established and new rows of houses built for their workforce, as the

FIG 3.2: *The vicarage of St Luke's church built around 1860 for a new parish, established a decade before to serve the increasing urban population. It features a Gothic porch, steep pitched roof and Elizabethan-style windows.*

town began to spread beyond its old centre. The railway arrived in 1849, although as at first its principal role was as a through route and for carrying goods there was no immediate effect on housing. New banks, shops and small businesses were established, their owners increasing the demand for refined detached houses, which Leek-based architects like William Sugden were commissioned to build. Despite the growing uniformity of building styles and materials across the country, it was still usual to employ a local architect for major works.

However, all this expansion had taken place without solving the basic problems of water supply and drainage. This came to a head in 1856 when there was 'a great mortality' in the town due to the lack of these services. The death rate was particularly high in the old crammed housing at the rear of the town centre, where up to ten houses were reported as sharing one privy! Improvement Commissioners bought the water works and extended the mains supply while a local mill owner and a surgeon paid for drinking water fountains. New drains were dug and sewage taken away, although at this date only to irrigate open fields on the edge of town before flowing back into the main river. These seemingly simple steps, though, dramatically lowered the death rate from thirty in a thousand to fifteen by the 1870s, and now even the poorest areas had access to a reliable water supply.

THE NATIONAL PICTURE

This was a boom period for much of the country as industry and agriculture benefited from the lack of competition from abroad. A rise in overall wealth and wages – even for the working classes with an increase of around 30% – meant better housing and this period saw improved quality, size and services in most types of building.

A reaction to global dominance was an insular attitude to the outside world. Young men travelled to the English colonies rather than on grand tours of Europe, and so were not influenced by the new fashions in architecture on the continent as their Georgian predecessors had been, but more by a glorification of our medieval past. The focus of the home also changed from one which looked out upon the community around it from lofty balconies, to an inward facing, protective environment for the family.

In the 1850s and 1860s there was a second boom in railway construction, especially of smaller, local lines linking into the national network. This created an opportunity for the railway companies and house builders to work together in developing the land around their new stations. These suburbs were particularly attractive to the growing middle classes who, benefiting from improved wages, aspired to be sole occupiers of a new house which imitated those of their social superiors, in an area far away from the filth in town and city centres. To maintain the exclusivity of these select estates, railway companies were known to only issue first-class tickets to the suburban stations so the undesirables would not be encouraged to settle there!

In the country, the boom in agriculture known as 'the Golden Age of Farming' resulted in landowners and farmers developing their estates. Efficient new farms were often arranged around a courtyard, with horse-powered machinery or, in the most up-to-date, a steam engine. Alongside these farms were new houses for the farmers, practical, solid-looking, detached houses reflecting their aspiration to be on an equal footing with the urban industrialist. There may

have been a steward's house close to the main farm buildings to keep an eye on the comings and goings of the labourers. Littered around the estate would be workers' cottages, single, semis and small terraces of brick or stone houses of a higher standard than most had been used to. In the dairy and sheep farming districts, where the coming of the railway meant meat and milk could be transported quickly to an eager market in the nearest town or city, the increased income could be ploughed back into housing. Those villages close to a railway also attracted new housing, principally for workers on the line or around the station, as well as new hotels and inns to serve the passing traffic.

FIG 3.3: *Country estate housing dating from the 1850s at Ilam in Staffordshire. Many villages were rebuilt with 'Olde English' style cottages throughout the 19th century by landlords with half an eye on impressing their guests! This example gives a foretaste of the Revival styles which were to become popular in urban areas in the 1870s and 1880s.*

The massive increase in housing over the past decades without any improvement in infrastructure caused problems which came to a head in the 1850s as epidemics, especially of cholera, devastated inner city areas and poor drainage resulted in foul odours. The most notable of these was London's Great Stink of 1856, which even caused the Houses of Parliament to be closed.

The 1848 Health Act, although only providing guidelines, enabled local authorities to pass byelaws and begin to improve sanitation. As in Leek, new drains and water supplies were laid on and access lanes to rear yards and courts had to be built for the removal of waste and ash. Privies began to be provided for individual houses and the livestock that the old country generation had brought with them into the yards were banned. Health was the order of the day and many of the improvements were based upon the limited but influential model housing movement to which notable philanthropists, including Prince Albert, made contributions.

THE STRUCTURE OF HOUSES IN THIS PERIOD

With growing health concerns, water supply and drainage became factors in the planning of houses. The kitchen or scullery, which would have required these supplies, was increasingly found in rear extensions rather than in the basement. Due to the potential damp problems and health concerns with these subterranean rooms, they were only common where land values were high and room tight. On the new, more spacious suburbs, there was plenty of depth in the plot for a suite of rooms to the rear. On medium-sized terraces, it was common for a privy to be built in a small lean-to on the end wall of the extension, but as they were either still of basic design or linked into a drainage system with no traps, they emitted foul odours. Windows were rarely fitted in the wall above them!

The rear extension reflected the new fashion for separating the family from the servants, with these service rooms preferably shut out behind a door at the end of the entrance passage. The rooms were often of lower ceiling height and it was common for there to be three storeys compared with two in the main house. It was also usual for them to be built in pairs, thus sharing a common side wall (cheaper to build and saving on heat). As they would usually

FIG 3.4: *From the 1850s bay windows and large panes of glass became more affordable; this example is from Ealing.*

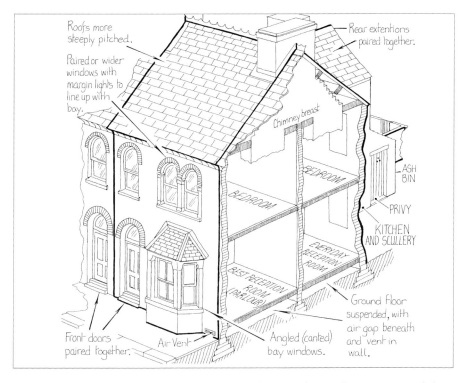

Roofs more steeply pitched.

Paired or wider windows with margin lights to line up with bay.

Rear extentions paired together.

Chimney breast

BEDROOM

BEDROOM

ASH BIN

PRIVY

KITCHEN AND SCULLERY

EVERYDAY RECEPTION ROOM

BEST RECEPTION ROOM (PARLOUR)

Ground floor suspended, with air gap beneath and vent in wall.

Front doors paired together.

Air Vent

Angled (canted) bay windows.

FIG 3.5: *A cut-away drawing of a medium-sized terrace house showing some of the new features which were popular in this period.*

be in line with the front door, this tied in with the fashion for pairing the entrances to terraced houses together (fig 3.6).

Cellars were still popular as they provided room for the storage of goods and coal, as well as some protection against rising damp, which was another important issue for house builders in this period. In houses without a cellar or basement, it became common to suspend the timber floor above the ground level by a foot or so and fit brick-size vents in the exterior walls to permit air to flow underneath. There was a small step up to the front door to reach the raised level. Other methods of inserting non-porous materials in the brickwork like sheets of slate were of mixed success; the most effective solution which came in later was to use dense engineering bricks for the bottom courses.

During the 1850s, the removal of the tax on the number of windows and duty on glass made the previously expensive bay window suddenly come within the means of a wider spectrum of people, and they became the must-have feature for any aspiring middle-class house! They could be straight sided or angled (canted) and could be capped by a sloping roof or flat parapet, depending on the style of the house, although at this date they tended only to appear on the ground floor. The repeal of the brick tax helped to reduce the cost of building taller houses and, at the same time, made the traditional English bond of brickwork, which was becoming popular again due to its use on 15th and 16th-century buildings, more affordable.

Large and Medium Houses

Rather than the regimented rows and sweeping crescents associated with Georgian and Regency housing, the new Victorian suburban estates contained the same variety and asymmetric aspects in their layout as they did in their design. This was often due to the old country lanes and features being retained and shaping the layout of the new developments, as well as to the popularity of detached villas and semis which broke up the monotony of classical façades. These new properties gave the owners more privacy and more space for the gardens which were becoming fashionable. In the case of large terraced houses, the old squares at the front overlooked by balconies were replaced by experimental arrangements, some with communal or separate private gardens running along the rear, which now that drainage was improving was less odorous. Facilities in the house were also improving with hot and cold water

now likely to be laid on, as well as gas for lighting.

Medium and Small Houses

Many of these improvements were featured in the smaller, terraced houses of white collar and industrial workers, where wages were sufficient to pay the higher rent. The houses were generally taller, with steeper pitched roofs in keeping with the Gothic trend and providing practical attic space. They were typically covered in slates but towards the end of the period machine-made tiles provided a cost effective alternative. The better two-bedroom house could feature a bay window and a rear extension, providing a kitchen and scullery below with an additional bedroom above. Further down the scale, small two-up two-downs and back-to-backs might benefit from local byelaws encouraging the provision of piped water, a privy for each house and improved rear access so waste could be removed, although this was hit and miss depending on the location. As with larger houses, it became normal to pair the front doors and rear extensions together in this period.

THE STYLE OF HOUSES

The eclectic mix of styles which was very much in evidence in the first decades of the Victorian period was to become crystallised into one particular form – the Gothic. Its proponents, including Pugin, argued that it was an indigenous style which provided reassuring continuity in the face of a rapidly changing industrial world. They also saw it as being morally superior,

FIG 3.6: *Terraced houses now had their front doors and rear extensions paired together. This example also shows how two thin flanking lights either side of the main first floor window were used to line up with the canted bay window below.*

coming from a medieval age which was believed to have been deeply religious and just, albeit through rose-tinted glasses! The most influential voice on the subject was that of John Ruskin who, in *The Stone of Venice*, criticised man and the machine and steered architecture back to the Gothic form on social and moral grounds. At the same time he laid the foundations for the next generation to reject the mass production on which the country's wealth was now built and embrace traditional, hand-made crafts.

Although the battle of styles which concerned architectural commentators may have been settled, the average villa, semi or terraced house was still likely to

be decorated in any one of three principal forms: the Gothic, Classical or Italianate, or as often happened with speculative builders, any combination of the three on the same building! They were restricted to some extent by the form of the window and door. Sash windows still dominated, now with larger panes, usually four in a typical window, although some fixed leaded lights or hinged casements were used on traditional-style buildings. The four-panelled door was common, some by the end of the period featuring glass in the upper two panels to let more light into the passage behind, while a variety of stylised forms, some with pointed tops, can be found particularly on the more expensive Gothic house.

Gothic

The archetypal Victorian red-brick Gothic house took form in this period, ranging from the large asymmetrical building with towers and steeply pitched roofs down to the modest terrace, with bay window and token pointed arch. In general, the builder tried to emphasise the vertical lines of the house, hence the pointed roofs, windows and doors. Decoration raised above the level of the surface was frowned upon so different coloured bricks were used to make patterns, ranging from simple bands across the façade to more elaborate designs above openings. Pointed gables, sometimes with decorated bargeboards (fig 3.3), were used even on terraces, where they could face outwards and break the horizontal line of the roof as an extension of the front or as a separate dormer window. Slate was still the most popular covering for the roof but now the top was capped by ridge tiles, some with sculptured crests featuring Gothic patterns or motifs. Windows and doors could have pointed arches above formed out of brickwork or whole window pieces made out of stone (or artificial materials) with narrow pointed openings (lancets). On smaller terraces, stone lintels might have a vaguely pointed carving on the underside with narrow columns featuring capitals, typically decorated with carved foliage, to the side, although many apparently

FIG 3.8: *A Gothic-style house from North Oxford, which was developed in the 1860s and 1870s. Note the pointed arches, steep gables facing the street and the polychromatic brickwork around the windows.*

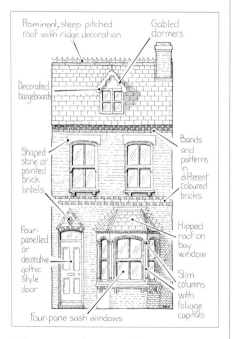

FIG 3.7: *An elevation of a medium-sized terrace house showing some of the subtle Gothic features which could be incorporated.*

Gothic houses still had round arched doorways or plain rectangular sash windows as the styles were mixed up.

Classical

The Classical form continued to be used, although principally in this period for important public buildings like town halls and banks. It was now universal for raised mouldings (aediculae), some with pilasters and pediments, to surround individual windows, rather than leaving them plain. Structural features like bay windows would be capped by a parapet hiding the roof, as was still typical at the top of the wall, although it would often be smaller with decorative brackets under the cornice and raised quoins at the corners of the building. Stone or stuccoed balustrades replaced ironwork along the front of balconies, which although less popular now tended to run across the whole façade with columns forming a porch or portico above the front door (a feature which more often now appeared on its own without the balcony).

Despite the strict forms of 18th-century Classicism being loosened, the builder still tried to line up the windows vertically. With the use of wider bay windows on the lower floors, they experimented with pairs of windows, or versions with margin lights to the side in order to keep the balance above. On smaller houses, plain lintels above rectangular windows and doors with pilasters or columns to their sides were popular. Another effect of the Gothic preaching of Pugin and Ruskin was to promote honesty in the materials used.

FIG 3.10: *A West London mid-Victorian Classical-style large terrace house. Note the two-storey canted bay windows with a parapet on top, the stuccoed ground floor and the more elaborate decoration around the doors and windows.*

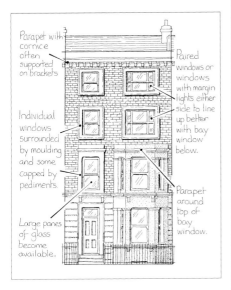

Parapet with cornice often supported on brackets

Paired windows or windows with margin lights either side to line up better with bay window below.

Individual windows surrounded by moulding and some capped by pediments.

Parapet around top of bay window.

Large panes of glass become available.

FIG 3.9: *Elevation of a medium/large terrace house in a Classical style showing some of the key features of this period.*

Therefore, stucco which could hide all manner of shortcuts and mistakes in construction fell from favour to leave good quality brickwork exposed, even on the most Classical houses. Stucco was still used, though, for the decorative features and sometimes covered the lower storey.

Italianate

The style of house based upon the Classical Italian Renaissance villa became very popular in the decade following its use for Queen Victoria and Prince Albert's country retreat, Osborne House. It was characterised by the use of round-headed openings, oversized, low pitched roofs with deep overhangs supported on brackets and, on larger houses, towers with flat pointed roofs and triple-arched openings below. Typically, windows were set in pairs, especially above a bay window in order to line up vertically. The round arch above the window could be moulded out of stone or stucco, or formed from different coloured brickwork.

FIG 3.12: *Classical-style large terrace houses in this period tended to feature a cornice or eaves with brackets, raised mouldings and pediments around the windows, continuous balconies including an extension supported upon columns over the door and stucco or stone balustrades rather than iron railings.*

FIG 3.11: *A west London house featuring Italianate features like the round-arched first floor twin windows and the flat-pitched hipped roof with brackets under the eaves.*

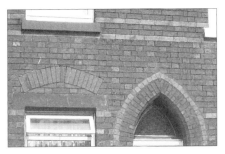

FIG 3.14: *On modest terrace houses Gothic details like pointed arches could simply be added within the brickwork or above a door.*

FIG 3.13: *An Italianate-style window, most commonly found in pairs.*

FIG 3.15: *A Victorian four-panelled exterior door. Although most had fielded panels top and bottom it had always been common for the bottom pair to be flush, to make them tougher and easier to clean where there was likely to be the most wear and tear.*

FIG 3.17: *A Gothic-style tripartite window with polychromatic brickwork and the surrounding wall in English bond, features popular in the 1860s and 1870s.*

FIG 3.16: *An Italianate sash window with the recess and pulley exposed above the upper sash.*

FIG 3.18: *In order to line up the first floor windows with the new bay below, two margin lights were added either side of the main first floor sash window, a very popular solution in the 1860s.*

FIG 3.19: *Italianate-style towers modelled upon campaniles (bell towers), with a shallow pitched pyramidal roof and two or three arched openings, sometimes featured on larger houses.*

FIG 3.20: *A mid-Victorian four-pane sash window. With only a few glazing bars, the frame joints at the bottom of the top sash had to be extended with the distinctive horns either side.*

CHAPTER 4

Late Victorian Houses 1870–1890

FIG 4.1: *Spout Hall, Leek, was designed by Richard Norman Shaw in 1871 and completed two years later. His inspiration was Cheshire timber-framed houses of the 16th and 17th century, blended with earlier Gothic doorways.*

The rapid growth of Leek in the first half of the Victorian period had resulted in poor housing and unhealthy living conditions. However, in this second half, the now influential factory owners turned their attention and not inconsiderable wealth to more benevolent causes, namely the health and well-being of their workers. When W. S. Brough built himself a new house on the outskirts of town in 1880, he had neighbouring land laid out as a park and separate recreation ground, while the Nicholson family built an institute, still bearing their name, which included a library and museum for the town. Others of means also contributed to the town. Adelina Alsop had the Cottage Hospital built in 1870 in memory of her husband, and Elizabeth Condlyffe bought land for almshouses, eight of which were erected on the site after her death in 1878.

Housing continued its gradual improvement and by the end of the 1880s more than half the population were living in more spacious two-up two-downs, while even the deprived areas in the town had running water and drainage. The land between the town and the railway station was developed and new exclusive houses began to appear, while the main roads were dis-turnpiked and the old tollhouses sold off for private residences. The Sugdens, Leek's most prominent architects, were busy adding new houses in a variety of styles to their growing portfolio. However, for the first time, houses were also being designed by notable architects from further afield like Richard Norman Shaw who designed Spout Hall for a local silk manufacturer in 1871 (fig 4.1). The town was growing in stature enough to attract other cultural heavyweights of the time including Oscar Wilde, George Bernard Shaw and William Morris, who worked with the local dyeworks owner, Thomas Wardle, to perfect new, natural fabric dyes.

THE NATIONAL PICTURE

The rather insular nature of Victorian Britain and its unrivalled industrial domination resulted in those of power and influence taking their eye off the ball – only to look out in this period and find boatloads of foreign manufactured goods and agricultural produce heading into our ports. The rest of the world was catching up and, in some cases, had begun to overtake us and the first place it was felt was in farming. Here the opening up of the American West led to an avalanche of cheap grain while new methods of refrigeration permitted meat to be shipped from all around the globe, resulting in an agricultural depression at home. Not all rural areas were affected

FIG 4.2: *A late Victorian villa with many of the characteristic features from this period: the roof with different patterned tiles, the spire capping the two-storey bay, the single-pane sash windows and terracotta plaques just under the eaves.*

FIG 4.3: *A middle-class terrace from Bedford Park which was developed in the 1880s and 1890s.*

as dairy farming, market gardening, fruit production and fishing benefited from our changing diet and the still increasing railway network. The country as a whole entered a period of boom and bust. Lower land rents crippled the already beleaguered aristocracy while successful financiers and the growing ranks of civil and public servants became more dominant and assertive. This social group found they had more buying power, not due to increases in wages but rather from lower priced goods as a result of foreign competition.

This inward-looking perspective was represented in the houses of the period. The new generation of architects, now numbering around ten times more than when Victoria came to the throne, had been brought up on a diet of Ruskin,

Pugin and Morris. Aided by a more detailed understanding of British architectural styles from the past, they set about re-working them into new forms. Their projects could now take them all over the country as it became more common for commissions for exclusive houses to be given to architects from outside the local area. New middle-class estates were seen as a worthwhile venture, most notably Bedford Park in London, where a number of leading architects were involved in designing fashionable Domestic Revival houses, aimed particularly at artisans.

Speculative builders, with access to a wider selection of architectural publications and detailed drawings, watered down many of these fashionable features and details onto the mass housing stock. With cheaper machine-made bricks, roof tiles and pre-cut stone embellishments (as these became harder to source terracotta pieces became popular) the builder could emulate superior buildings at little extra cost. Now, for the first time, those higher paid workers from the lower classes, factory foremen and skilled workers, were moving into new estates in the suburbs – although they preferred the tram to the socially restrictive train!

Health issues still dominated housing developments. In this later Victorian period sanitation was the watchword. Manufacturers produced modern sanitary wares, from drainpipes and traps to new designs of water closet, making the environs of the house more pleasant and the garden more inviting.

Those further down the ladder benefited from continued improvements in water supply and sewerage although, even by 1890, there were cities and towns where around one in five families did not have running water in their house. Although the vast majority still rented their houses, those in high wage areas began to buy their homes with the aid of the new building societies, while others less well off could benefit from purchasing schemes run by the likes of the Co-operative movement.

THE STRUCTURE OF HOUSES

In the later Victorian house, balconies from which to gaze upon the goings on outside were redundant. Instead, the garden at the rear, communal or private, became its focus. For larger houses, brick and stone walls with decorated or plain capped pillars either side of a gated entrance made a prominent statement about the owner's desire for privacy, enforced by a mask of rhododendrons and exotic trees. Inside a visitor might be kept waiting in the hall, where a chair was a common piece of furniture, the rooms leading off being principally the private domain of the family, with the servants equally segregated at the rear.

In general, houses became larger – many taller, some wider, although generally it was with further extensions at the back that extra rooms were created. Roofs remained steeper than in the first half of the century, the pitch and design reflecting the style of house. Gothic roofs were generally pointed, with exposed gables

facing out, while hipped roofs were popular on Queen Anne-style buildings. Cheaper mass-produced roof tiles made a cost effective alternative to slates and offered a wider choice of patterns and colours. It became popular to lay the roof out with alternate bands of different shaped and coloured tiles and slates. In the hands of revivalist architects the chimney arose from obscurity and became a prominent feature once more, with huge brick stacks complementing the historic style of house.

Large and Medium Houses

These became larger still in this period, to accommodate new service rooms, more bedrooms, a nursery and, in some, a plumbed-in bathroom. In the suburbs and country, large houses spread out and nestled into the landscape rather

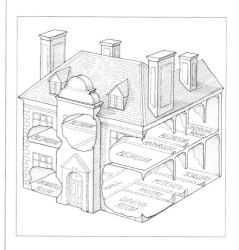

FIG 4.4: *A cut-out of a detached house in Queen Anne-style.*

than dominating it, hiding behind a curtain of foliage to protect privacy and in wariness of the now enfranchised working classes.

The designers of this new generation of exclusive houses had to allow for improved conditions for servants and a more hierarchical structure. They provided halls for dining with separate rooms for the housekeeper and butler. As the servants were kept further from sight than before, their rooms typically had to be placed in larger rear extensions, as basement rooms were frowned upon owing to health concerns. The family living in the larger houses would expect a main dining room and separate breakfast or morning room, a library for the master and, in some, even a billiards or smoking room, with perhaps the dining room and library overlooking the rear garden. The exotic plants grown required suitable housing so conservatories were fashionable features attached or freestanding close by. The most notable new arrivals in this period were the bathroom and water closet, which although existing in some houses before were now a standard feature in many large and medium-sized houses; both were typically very small at this date. Separate bedrooms for boys and girls had been standard

FIG 4.5: *A middle-class terraced house with a cut out exposing a possible arrangement of the interior.*

for a while but now a nursery, usually south-facing to receive the maximum light, was fitted in.

The top end of medium-sized terrace houses grew in stature with higher ceilings over their two or three floors. The attic above was illuminated by dormers and increased space was created by larger, rear extensions. The ground-floor bay window, which had become the must-have fashion accessory of the 1860s, was by the 1880s extended up to the main bedroom above. There were restrictions in the depth that the bay could protrude from the façade and so bays could be square-sided as well as angled. With cellars, but rarely basements, below, the kitchen, scullery, coal sheds and water closet were fitted in the rear extension. Now it was becoming more common for houses in this class to have hot as well as cold water, with a heated copper often sited in the scullery or kitchen.

Medium and Small Houses

Once exclusive features were now filtering down to more modest housing. The two or three-bedroom terraced house could have a hall leading off the front door, a bay window on the ground floor and, best of all, a parlour at the front. This was an exclusive room for special occasions which the working classes aspired to. The gradual increase in wages and reduced cost of products helped the less skilled and fortunate raise their expectations of housing. Although back-to-backs were still built (with improved quality, size and services) the small two-up two-down house with

through passageways and rear yards came within the reach of more people. More effective legislation forced builders and authorities to ensure that each property had a separate water or earth closet, ash bins, coal stores and proper access lanes at the rear for the removal of waste.

Most now had running cold water and efficient drainage while some may have even had a copper for hot water and a small range for cooking. It would be a long time before bathrooms were built into this size of house but some had tubs fitted under the floorboards of the scullery or rear living room, which could be exposed at the weekly or monthly bath time!

FIG 4.6: *A later Gothic-style house featuring outward facing gables over two-storey bays with decorated bargeboards and steeply pointed roof and porch.*

THE STYLE OF HOUSES IN THIS PERIOD

The mass of middle and working-class terrace housing was still influenced by Gothic or Classical styling or mixes of both on their now larger and more structurally interesting forms. Generally, the Gothic house would still have a steeper pitched roof but now with patterns made out of the different shaped and coloured tiles, terracotta ridge decoration and the triangular gable above the full height bay or dormer windows facing out to the street. Sash windows were still used in this class of house but now more often with full-sized panes in the two frames and no glazing bars.

Although some larger houses were built in the vertical Gothic style or the more horizontal Classical, the new generation of architects were generally disinterested in the old moral squabbles between these two forms. They were more concerned with rejecting the mass-produced culture in favour of conjuring up new styles which embraced the beauty and the uniqueness of traditional crafts.

Domestic Revival

Whereas the Gothic of the mid-Victorian period was inspired by 14th and 15th-century church architecture, the new English Revival style looked to the more humble houses of the Tudor

FIG 4.7: *Features of a late Victorian terraced house.*

FIG 4.8: *Revival-style houses dating from the 1880s with mock timber framing, mullioned windows and decorative bargeboards.*

and Elizabethan period. Mock timber framing, hand-made bricks, fine cut stone, tile hanging, pebbledash and traditional roof coverings came back into fashion as the influence of what was to become labelled the Arts and Crafts movement and its rejection of industrial production encouraged a return to vernacular methods. The largest houses were designed to appear as if they had developed over centuries, with wandering layouts, asymmetrical shapes and a medley of different exterior materials, while above there were huge sweeping roofs finished with decorative bargeboards.

The terraces and semis of the middle classes were also influenced by these vernacular styles as a new generation of prospective tenants chose houses with humble cottage features rather than ones which tried to emulate a country house. Many of the details which architects used on exclusive detached houses found their way down to the speculative stock, with plain façades broken up by tile hanging, mock timber work and plain or fretted bargeboards. The corner stones (quoins) of the structure were often highlighted by using contrasting masonry and English bond brickwork which had been common in the 16th century was revived, while carved stone and terracotta panels and motifs were inserted into the façade for decoration. By this time there were problems with the availability and rising cost of stone in certain areas of the country. From the 1870s, builders started to use terracotta for decoration as well as an increasing range of other applications. The ancient recipe for terracotta had been lost and it

was only in the 1840s that a new method of moulding a purified, fine grained clay and firing it to over 1,000 degrees was discovered. Ridge tiles and chimney pots were among its early uses on houses, but in this period its popularity boomed and catalogues full of decorative panels, mouldings, window and door heads were available to builders.

The Classical four-panelled door and large sheet glass sash windows were often inappropriate in this style of rustic house, so a variety of more humble, planked doors and casement windows were used. However, the sash window

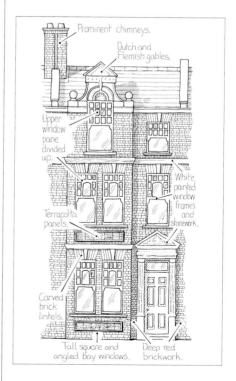

FIG 4.9: *A Queen Anne-style façade.*

Prominent chimneys.

Dutch and Flemish gables.

Upper window pane divided up.

White painted window frames and stonework.

Terracotta panels.

Carved brick lintels.

Tall square and angled bay windows.

Deep red brickwork.

was cheaper at this date so to solve the problems with its appearance, on a tighter budget, leaded lights or wooden glazing bars were used to break it up. A successful compromise which became popular from the 1880s was to use these features on the top sash but keep the lower one clear.

Queen Anne

The architects involved in the Revival movement rose to prominence as they worked on a wider range of exclusive estates and individual commissions all over the country. The most influential architect of domestic architecture was Richard Norman Shaw. He helped to develop a style inspired by elements of 17th-century Dutch houses which, being popular in late 17th and early 18th-century England, were associated with the reigns of William and Mary and then Anne, hence the adoption of the label 'Queen Anne'. They notably featured Dutch and Flemish gables (composite forms of curves and triangles) and hipped roofs with a prominent chimney. Most refreshing was the use of red-brick and painted white woodwork, as up until then it had been common for windows and doors to be painted in dark colours or grained in a wood effect. Casement

and oriel windows were popular, with the top sections broken up by leaded lights or glazing bars. This Queen Anne style proved popular as its forms could be replicated easily and cheaply onto the terraced houses of the middle classes.

FIG 4.10: *Late Victorian semis with Queen Anne-style features like the Dutch gables, white painted sash windows with sub-divided upper parts, cut brick lintels and the use of rich red-brickwork.*

FIG 4.11: *Even on modest houses in this period, chimneys could feature terracotta mouldings or a shaped structure in a period style, simple pierced ridge tiles and decorated bargeboards, as in these two examples.*

FIG 4.14: *Terracotta was the fashionable accessory of this period, formed into plaques, tiles, datestones, and moulded parts as in these four examples below. It was usually unglazed although the elaborately structured oriel window in the bottom right has glazed parts in contrast to the rich red-brick.*

FIG 4.12: *Shaped gables, white horizontal features, sashes with divided upper parts, tiled roofs and hanging decorative tiles all feature on this Queen Anne-style house.*

FIG 4.15: *Stone cross windows (with vertical mullions and horizontal transoms) featuring leaded lights made a return on Domestic Revival houses.*

FIG 4.13: *Later Victorian exterior doors had much more variety reflecting the style of house; the left-hand one is from a Queen Anne house, the middle and right-hand are in a Revival style.*

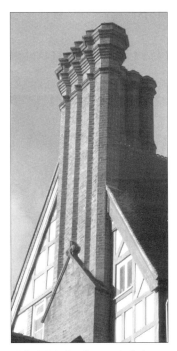

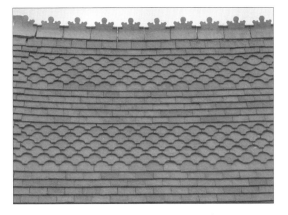

FIG 4.17: *Roofs in this period were often patterned, either with different coloured machine tiles or with bands of alternate shaped slates or tiles, and were still usually capped by terracotta decorative ridge tiles.*

FIG 4.16: *In this period the chimney became an important and prominent part of large house design, as with these 16th-century style brick stacks on a mock timber-framed Revival house.*

FIG 4.19: *Despite the increasing range of period windows for Revival houses, the most common form was still the sash window, now often with a single sheet of glass, although by the 1880s the top sash was sometimes subdivided by glazing bars.*

FIG 4.18: *Turrets, towers and full height bays were common in this period, usually capped by types of squat spires.*

CHAPTER 5

The Last Decade and Beyond 1890–1901

FIG 5.1: *A row of middle-class terraced houses on Westwood Road, Leek, overlooking a recreation ground in an area which was developed in the 1890s. These cheerful houses have walled front gardens, white painted timber work, bands of patterned brick and bargeboards on the dormer windows. Continuous porches over the ground floor window and door, sculptured chimneys and the patterned glazing bars in the top sash of the window are all features typical of this period.*

Houses of steadily improving quality continued to be built in Leek during these closing years of Victoria's reign, from new Arts and Crafts structures and imposing four-storey semis to further straight rows of working class terraces, now enlivened by small bays and discrete decoration. In between were fine red-brick, two and three storey, middle class houses for the still growing numbers of skilled and white collar workers. The new urban district council was now responsible for the services previously performed by the improvement commissioners and other bodies, but as yet was not involved in providing housing, which was still principally in the hands of landlords.

This was a problem for those on the bottom rung of the social ladder. The drive for better health had led to the clearance of the worst slums, resulting in a shortage of housing. The new, improved houses being erected were also too expensive for them to rent. It was private enterprise that tried to remedy the situation, the most notable individual being James Cornes who, in 1901, erected fifty specially-designed homes which even included bathrooms, for working families.

By the turn of the 20th century, Leek had changed dramatically from the small market town it had been when Victoria came to the throne some sixty years earlier. Huge mill complexes dominated the centre of town, driving the population from around 6,000 in the 1830s to more than 15,000 in 1901. Those who had found success in business were no longer living in the plain Georgian terraces in town but had moved into mock timber-framed villas hidden amongst greenery on the outskirts. Their foremen and skilled staff could now expect roomy two and three-bedroom houses which, unlike the plain and monotonous terraces of fifty years earlier now featured double bay windows, timber-clad gables and the luxury of gas and hot water. The majority of workers had gone from single room accommodation and tiny

FIG 5.2: *A row of houses in Langford Street, Leek, which were erected specifically for working families by James Cornes in 1901. This was due to a housing shortage partly caused by the clearing of poor housing and rising rents. Not only were they more spacious and decorative but they also had a bathroom, a luxury at this date.*

squalid houses to larger two-up two-downs, with water, drainage, and their own privy. This was a vast improvement on what had gone before, but still a long way from the standard demanded today.

THE NATIONAL PICTURE

When Queen Victoria was laid to rest in 1901, she left behind a still powerful nation. However, growth was stagnant, with cycles of boom and bust due to competition from abroad. This had forced our percentage of worldwide manufactured goods to fall from over 25% to under 20% in just a few decades. Her Empire had reached its peak in area, yet despite the contact with such diverse cultures the nation still preferred to look inwards and

FIG 5.3: *Port Sunlight, Birkenhead: Four examples from this exceptional estate village built in the 1890s and early 1900s for workers from the Sunlight Soap Factory. Architects, including a young Sir Edwin Lutyens, were employed to design houses in a wide range of styles to include features like Dutch gables (left), low slung roofs (middle left), elongated mullion windows with leaded lights (middle right) and continuous roofs over bay window and door (right).*

was not popular until improved light bulbs arrived in 1907). Hot and cold running water was more widespread but still not common until after the Second

backwards, with architects and builders at their most confident when delving into their historic toolbox of parts. If continental styles were used it was more likely to be old Gothic details rather than the fashionable Art Nouveau. This movement was very influential in Europe at the time, but only appeared here in decorative glass and interior fittings.

The 1890s and 1900s were marked by a building boom which helped still further to reduce the number of people living in overcrowded conditions yet, at the same time, left us with houses of arguably the finest quality. Most of these had gas and some electricity (although it

FIG 5.4: *Some of the distinctive features of a mid-sized terrace house from this period.*

World War. The newly-formed district and county councils had little to do with housing at this stage. It was still down to benevolent private individuals and factory owners to provide better housing for the working classes, as at Port Sunlight on the Wirral, Bourneville south of Birmingham and New Earswick, near York.

THE STRUCTURE OF HOUSES IN THIS PERIOD

The houses erected in the last decade of the 19th century and first decade of the 20th showed the same variety in layout and structure as had been the hallmark of earlier Victorian architecture, although their appearance had become crystallised upon the revival of English 16th and 17th-century styles. Large houses could vary from elongated two-storey structures overshadowed by huge, low-slung roofs, to imposing terraces and semis of a height never since built in domestic architecture. Middle-class houses were also generally larger, including space for a small bathroom while outside a small front and private rear garden enhanced rural aspirations. Back-to-backs were still being erected in a few industrial cities. However, most new working-class housing was in the form of a two-up two-down through house with a rear yard and sometimes a small rear extension providing extra space. At the same time, experiments with new layouts of houses were starting to appear offering a wider plot and the more familiar 20th-century form.

One of the distinctive changes on a façade in this period was created by the 1894 Building Act which relaxed the rules on recessing windows. Since the Great Fire of London, ever stricter regulations had seen the window-frame recessed further back and behind the outside wall. However, with few timber-framed and thatched houses in towns by the end of the 19th century, the risk of fire had been greatly reduced. With the re-introduction of casement

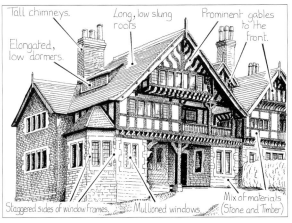

Tall chimneys.

Long, low slung roofs

Prominent gables to the front.

Elongated, low dormers.

Staggered sides of window frames. Mullioned windows. Mix of materials (Stone and Timber)

FIG 5.5: *A Cheshire Revival-style house showing the features which were popular at the time.*

63

windows in Revival houses, projecting wooden window frames had already reappeared, but after this act it became a widespread fashion. It was now common in both casement and sash windows for the top half or third to be divided up by glazing bars in a variety of patterns or with leaded lights incorporating stained glass. This helped the window to fit in with the style of the façade, while at the same time allowed a clear view through the single pane below when looking out.

The use of timber around doors had also been limited in the past. It is another distinctive feature of this period to find long roofs stretching over the ground floor bay window square and front door, supported by timber brackets and sometimes incorporating decorative woodwork. Stretcher bond brickwork, in which the inner and outer skins are held together by metal ties across the cavity, became more common, although its use depended upon regions and

styling. On some larger houses, and even on the ends of smaller rows, brick and stone turrets were added, a fashionable accessory in the 1880s and 1890s, capped with a pointed roof or squat spire.

Large and Medium Houses

As it had become harder to retain servants in houses with poor conditions, the basement became rare in upper and middle-class houses except where the cost of the building plot or lie of the land made it worthwhile. Bathrooms were now more common in large and medium-sized houses, although surprisingly many of the rich were not keen on them as they still had servants to make up their bath so didn't need new fangled plumbing!

THE STYLE OF HOUSES IN THIS PERIOD

The Domestic Revival styles were the most influential upon the houses built in this period. From the large sprawling

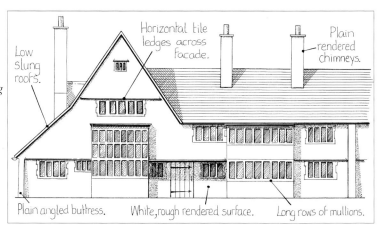

FIG 5.6: *An Arts and Crafts-style house with some of its distinguishing features.*

Low slung roofs.

Horizontal tile ledges across facade.

Plain rendered chimneys.

Plain angled buttress.

White, rough rendered surface.

Long rows of mullions.

detached buildings down to the modest terrace, vernacular materials and fashions were revived to decorate their exteriors. Although mass-produced goods were now available nationwide, the exclusive housing found inspiration and materials locally with, for instance, black and white decorative timber framing in Cheshire and the use of clunch, a hard chalk, in the Chilterns. Further down the building stock, speculative builders were embellishing their standard terraced structures with timber patterned gables, hanging tiles, projecting windows, single or double bays, decorative stained glass, pebbledash and plain renders.

Gothic houses were still being built, notably red-brick structures with steeply pitched roofs and turrets, while Classical styles still influenced housing, especially those from the late 17th century which Norman Shaw had made popular in the 1880s. Many of the decorative pieces which were available in the catalogues for builders were still in medieval or ancient styles, so rows of terraces continued to be erected with Gothic and Classical themes. These off-the-shelf, mass-produced building parts were anathema to the new generation of revivalists who, from the late 1890s, were considered part of the Arts and Crafts movement.

Arts and Crafts Movement

The Arts and Crafts movement had been taking shape since the 1850s through the inspiration of cultural leaders like John Ruskin, William Morris and the new generation of Domestic Revival architects of the

FIG 5.7: *Some of the features found on Arts and Crafts houses. Pargeting (Art Nouveau-style elongated flowers) on the left, an angled buttress with pebbledash in the middle and circular chimneys again with pebbledash on the right.*

1870s and 1880s. It rejected mass production and sought to revive hand crafts and the use of local materials, although, unlike the architects of the past two decades, its notable proponents created new personal styles and forms, which at first glance appear to have more in common with 20th-century architecture than Olde English. In fact, it was the work of architects in this period like C. F. A. Voysey, M. H. Baillie Scott and Edwin Lutyens which were later copied by the builders of 1920s and 1930s semi-detached suburbia.

Arts and Crafts architects used local stones, hand-made bricks and regional styles of surface decoration like tile hanging, pebbledash, pargeting, wooden shingles and timber framing. There was more emphasis on the horizontal than the vertical, as houses spread out rather than stood tall. Mullioned windows (a simple opening divided up by vertical mullions to hold the leaded glass in place) were re-introduced, set in long rows with the sides formed by separate stones with a staggered edge. Roofs were often long and low slung, hipped with large gables facing forwards, while some were even thatched. A notable feature of Arts and Crafts houses is that the architects' influence extended beyond just the structure. Some designed details

ranging from wallpapers, fabrics and tiles down to the hinges for the doors.

Although inspired by the socialist ideals of its leaders like William

FIG 5.10 (above): *Pairs of chimneys were often sited directly over the front and rear fireplaces, in effect appearing halfway down the slope of the roof, in the last decade of the 19th century.*

FIG 5.8 (above): *Stained glass in the upper portions of windows was a popular form of decoration from the 1880s onwards.*

FIG 5.9 (below): *Mock Tudor chimneys and decorative terracotta mouldings remained popular in this period.*

FIG 5.11 (below): *A house dating from the turn of the century featuring period details like the casement windows standing slightly proud of the wall now fire regulations had been relaxed, brick lintels above windows with divided top sashes and the use of mock timber framing on the gable.*

FIG 5.12: *Continuous porches running over a bay window and door were common in this period. Note the front doors with stained glass upper parts, a popular feature in the last decades of Victoria's reign.*

Morris, Arts and Crafts houses and goods, by their very nature not mass-produced, remained expensive and did not reach or influence their intended market. Many became disillusioned with it or ended up in financial ruin. The movement ran out of impetus by the early 1900s, although ironically its style rather than its reliance upon hand crafts was to influence the mass housing of the later garden cities and inter-war suburbia.

SUMMARY

In the sixty-four years since Queen Victoria came to the throne, her kingdom had changed from a rural-based economy in which half the people still lived in the countryside to an industrial giant, with 80% residing in towns and cities. The old aristocracy, with their wealth built upon rents from their estates had been progressively weakened and it was the new breed of gentlemen, who had made their fortune in industry and finance, who were now the patrons of artists and architects. The middle classes had also emerged as an influential force, demanding more distinguished housing in order to emulate their social superiors, although in 1901 they still made up less than 15% of the population.

The remainder of the working population had benefited from a progressive rise in wages through the Victorian period. At the turn of the century, the poor could expect a house with four rooms compared with only one or two rooms within a shared property in 1837. Most levels in society could view their house as a significant improvement on that lived in by their great-grandparents. It was probably larger, better quality and certainly better equipped, and yet few actually owned them as nearly nine out of ten people still rented in 1901.

THE VICTORIAN HOUSE SINCE 1901

Over the last 100 years, the fashionable shortcomings of the largest houses and intolerable conditions in most of the smallest have seen the destruction of much of this Victorian housing stock. However, the good quality, sufficiently spacious and versatile middle-class buildings with their lively façades and colourful detailing have survived and thrived as they have become fashionable once again in the owner-occupier age.

The very largest houses were the first to go, as the rising costs of death duties and super tax, falling incomes and the loss of heirs in the First World War resulted in the abandonment of many country and urban mansions. At the same time, there began a sudden opening of the eyes to continental fashion and the appearance of an international style whose stark, plain horizontal forms made the grimy, brick Victorian Gothic pile seem out of date, especially in the modernist euphoria after the Second World War.

The back-to-backs and other small houses, whatever their structural qualities or deficiencies, were always on borrowed time as they had been so poorly and tightly laid out. They had no gardens or proper road access and many remained hotbeds of disease and deprivation. It was not until the 1950s and 1960s, with the building of council houses and high-rise flats that these potential slum areas could be removed. Today there are only fragmented examples of the buildings which once housed the majority of the Victorian working population.

The housing stock in the middle, from the large Classical or Gothic villa down to the rows of two-up two-down terraces, has often survived, thanks to better quality construction and planning, although most have changed to meet modern requirements over the century. Coal fires had always limited the size of the room to the space they could heat. With the introduction of central heating and gas fires, the ground floor could be opened out with the dividing wall between the front and rear rooms most commonly being turned into an arch to create a through sitting room and dining room. It was also possible to create a modern kitchen in the rear extension, while a room above could easily be converted into a bathroom.

Outside though, there has been less room for improvement. The roads, which were never designed for cars, have become congested with parked vehicles. Even some of the better middle-class houses never had enough space at the front to create off-road parking, whilst the small yard at the back limits the budding gardener in their scope. These factors have in the past kept many areas of Victorian housing at the bottom end of the modern housing stock.

However, in the past twenty years there has been a negative reaction to the modern style of housing erected in the 1950s and 1960s. The Victorian terrace, semi and villa, with their better quality materials, patterned brickwork, elaborate decoration and now rusticated appearance have become desirable residences and are at last receiving the restoration their glorious, flamboyant exteriors are worthy of.

FIG 5.13: *The Black Country Museum, Dudley, West Midlands. One of a handful of places where reconstructed Victorian houses can be seen in an original form with fully fitted interiors. These working-class houses date from the late Victorian period (note the chimneys halfway down the roof).*

SECTION II

THE
VICTORIAN
HOUSE IN
DETAIL

CHAPTER 6

General Fittings and Decoration

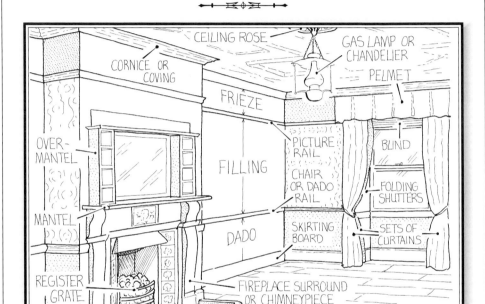

FIG 6.1: *A principal reception room with its general fittings.*

The interior of most houses was transformed during the Victorian age from a purely functional arrangement of limited furnishings, to one in which the owners could express their appreciation of style and displays of wealth. This was especially true of the growing middle classes. With the opening of notable buildings to the public and new galleries, museums and libraries the middle classes discovered an appreciation of the arts and with their increased income had the funds to purchase it (albeit reproductions). Even the working classes could aspire to interiors designed for more than just function. When social improving groups provided the poorer classes with what were intended as two everyday living rooms, the owners often designated one as a parlour, filled it with the best furniture they could afford and reserved it for special occasions, while they endured cramped conditions in the remaining room.

As with the exterior of the house, there was a massive array of styles from the Classical and Exotic of the early years to the Revivalists and Arts and Crafts at the close of the century. It was even permissible in the 1830s and 1840s to mix the styles up within the same house, so you could find Gothic-inspired decoration next to Arabesque.

Unlike today, the interiors of middle and upper class Victorian houses had to accommodate servants ranging in number from one for a humble clerk to as many as fifteen in the largest town houses. The rooms in which they worked, ate and slept were positioned to keep them out of view and maintain the respectable Victorian's obsession with privacy. They were also treated with a lower status of decoration than those of the family. This hierarchy of decoration also applied to the remaining rooms in the house with those like the hall and principal reception room liable to receive the most lavish adornment to impress upon visitors the owner's wealth and

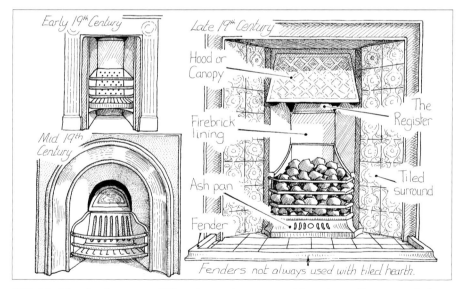

FIG 6.2: *The development of Victorian register grates. Note the earliest example has a perforated back plate to allow air into the fire, and the next example in the distinctive mid to late arched casting has grooves in the firebrick lining to achieve the same effect. Later types restricted the air flow to allow the fire to burn evenly and hence produce less smoke, so the underside was either blocked or fitted with an ash pan with a sliding vent.*

good taste. Bedrooms, even for the master and mistress of the house, would be spartan in comparison. It is important to bear this in mind when trying to recognise the original use of rooms in a house or when choosing appropriate decoration if restoring it. It is also worth noting that the majority of housing which was for the working classes was devoid of decoration fitted by the builder, with only a basic fireplace surround and perhaps coving or skirting for the walls in the better or later examples.

FIREPLACES

An essential feature in a room for both function and display was the fireplace. Not only was it the source of heat, but its surround and mantle gave ample opportunity for decoration, making it the focal point of the room.

Grates

The most important part of a Victorian fireplace was its cast-iron grate in which the coals were held. These had evolved as coal grew in popularity as a fuel by the end of the 18th century, with improved transportation. As coal burns better in a compact mass, the early grates were small, freestanding baskets. This was improved upon with the fixed hob grate, which had two rectangular plates either side of the coals upon which kettles could be heated.

However, these simple designs were inefficient, losing heat up the chimney and creating draughts in the room. In 1797 an American, Benjamin Rumford, suggested certain improvements to reflect more heat into the room and improve the flow of air into the fire. These included narrowing the throat of the flue and reducing the size of the fireplace, lowering the basket and bringing it forward, and angling the sides. However, we were slow to take up these ideas and it wasn't until the mid 19th century that many of them were put into practice.

A development which had appeared in the mid 1700s was to fit an adjustable damper called a register at the entrance to the flue, in order to control the draw of the fire. By the early Victorian period, register grates which included the metal basket which holds the coals, dampers and sometimes even a basic surround often cast all in one piece were becoming popular. In the 1850s, arched topped versions became

FIG 6.3: *A late Victorian register grate with an integrated cast-iron hood and tiled surround.*

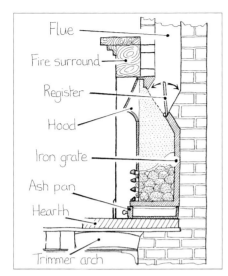

Flue
Fire surround
Register
Hood
Iron grate
Ash pan
Hearth
Trimmer arch

FIG 6.4: *A section through a fireplace showing the hinged register which controlled the draw up the chimney. Due to the weight of the grate and surround a trimmer arch may be fitted beneath the floorboards for support.*

fashionable with the basket lowered and firebrick linings as recommended by Rumford, the latter move designed to improve combustion. By the 1870s this had been taken a stage further by reducing the speed at which the fire burns with the addition of a firebrick and later an ash pan under the fire to reduce or, with the addition of a sliding vent, control the rate of combustion. This became important as the amount of smoke being produced was alarming certain quarters and a fire which burns more completely and evenly creates less pollution. Consumption of coal in London alone had grown four times in only 30 years; the Great Fog of 1880,

caused by coal fires, killed around 700 people.

The style changed to a rectangular opening casting with splayed sides covered with tiles, which not only reflected the heat but provided an opportunity for decoration. In the 1880s the fire was being brought further into the room to reduce heat loss so a small and sometimes adjustable hood or canopy was fitted above it to keep the smoke out.

There were many variants of register grates. Those with smoke-consuming grates tried to introduce fuel to the bottom of the fire to reduce the smoke problem. Complex hot air grates brought conducted air from an external source around the fire and out through vents or perforations around the arched or square opening.

FIG 6.5: *A marble fireplace surround with a Tudor four-centred arched opening, tiled splayed sides and a register grate.*

Traditional dog and hob grates were still used and wood burning fires, with firedogs holding the logs within a large opening, were often found in pseudo-medieval and Tudor houses. Gas fires were introduced in the later 19th century but they were expensive, unreliable and made little impression at this date.

Fire Surround

The Victorian fire surround or chimney piece varied in both style and material; the style to suit the theme of decoration and the material on funds and the status of the room. They could differ from marble and hardwood surrounds in the principal reception rooms of the larger houses, to slate, cast-iron and

FIG 6.6: *A late Victorian/Edwardian cast-iron one-piece fireplace surround and grate.*

softwoods in lesser rooms or houses. Plain wooden versions were stained or painted for servants' quarters or working-class houses. The size of the surround was determined by the size of the room. The designs chosen for the principal rooms varied dramatically, from massive elaborate pieces to plain and practical. As with most fittings in Victorian houses, softwoods, metal, plaster and cheaper stone were always stained or painted in some form or other to imitate a superior material. A waxed or varnished pine would never have been used.

The Regency and early Victorian fire surround tended to be a flat, rectangular frame with decorative mouldings applied to the surface. The most characteristic of the time had a round feature in the top corners and reeding down the sides (jambs). Marble, hard and softwoods and plaster structures were decorated and shaped with Classical, early Gothic and exotic details. By the mid-Victorian period more ornate surrounds were popular with large foliage brackets supporting what was becoming a deeper mantelpiece to accommodate the increasing number of ornaments which it was fashionable to collect and display. Large marble or paint effect slate was common around the arched topped register grates and Gothic-styled stone surrounds, with a flat pointed arch opening and ecclesiastical decorations, were appropriate for the mock Tudor house. Later, surrounds had to accommodate more clutter than before so overmantels were fitted above them, a common type comprising boxed-in shelves up each side with a large mirror

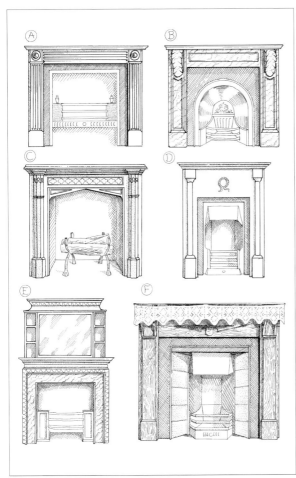

FIG 6.7: *A selection of Victorian fireplace surrounds. (A) is Regency/ early Victorian with distinctive fluted or ribbed jambs and lintel and circular medallions in the corners. (B) is a marble mid-Victorian fireplace with brackets supporting the mantle shelf, and (C) is a stone, Gothic-style surround of similar date. (D) is a single piece cast-iron surround and grate, typically used in bedrooms or cheaper housing while (E) is a later Victorian piece in an early 18th-century style but with an overmantel featuring a mirror and shelving. (F) shows a simple stained wood late 19th-century surround with tiles, register grate and a smoke deflector hanging over the mantle shelf; these originally were used to reduce smoke coming back into the room but at this date they became popular purely as a decorative piece.*

between. Now that plate glass was widely available this style became more affordable. Cast-iron surrounds, painted to imitate stone or just blackened were now more acceptable even in the best rooms, while the increase in the cost of marble made black or grey slates a popular cheap alternative.

The rejection of all things mass-produced by Arts and Crafts designers saw them recommend the use of wood rather than coal. Old firedogs and large opening fireplaces were designed in some of their houses. These included inglenook fireplaces, with seating within the recess and elaborately designed medieval, Oriental and Renaissance-styled surrounds, usually with an

FIG 6.8: *Beaten and polished copper hoods were popular in the last years of the century.*

overmantel. In the most up-to-date interior there was a rejection of ornamentation and plain tiled or brick covered surrounds or chimney breasts dwarfing an inserted grate were often designed. Beaten and polished copper was popular in the 1890s, usually for hoods fitted above the grate opening while cast-iron surrounds were

FIG 6.9: *A late Victorian black marble-effect surround with a tiled register grate and brass accessories.*

burnished silver as well as blackened. The tiles which were popular up the slips and sometimes on the cast-iron hoods at the time gave the Arts and Crafts or Art Nouveau designer further scope for decoration.

Chimney and Flue

The chimney stack, and the flues within, were usually built in brick, even in stone areas, with separate stacks in terraces built with the party wall as the rear and then, in the second half of the century, more often back-to-back as doors and chimneys were paired. In the most basic terraces, the stack takes the shape of a tuning fork with the chimney as the handle at the top. In larger houses there was a greater variety of arrangements and with the large number of flues the stack itself could grow wider on each floor to accommodate them. Despite the image of children as chimney sweeps in this period, their use was actually banned in 1829. By the 1850s the improved design of fireplaces had resulted in a narrower flue (around nine to ten inches square) which would have prohibited children going up them in new houses anyway.

Usually the number of pots on the chimney matches the number of fireplaces originally fitted. Not every room had a fireplace at first, often a small bedroom or servants' quarters might have missed out. Chimney pots appeared from the turn of the 19th century to improve the draw and reduce down-draughts. There was a wide range of terracotta and ceramic pots in simple designs in the mid 1800s, which evolved to more elaborate and imitation

Elizabethan-types by the 1870s and became a distinctive feature of Victorian housing. There were various adaptations to the top of the pot and a variety of metal cowls and deflectors which could be added, all intended to reduce the down-draught problem, with mixed results.

STAIRS

There is no standard position for stairs in Victorian houses. In larger terraced housing they were usually positioned up against the party wall towards the rear. Guests could admire the elaborate balustrades and posts, yet the owner only had to pay for one side and when out of sight upstairs it could fall back to a cheaper, simpler design. Smaller terraces with no hallway often have the stairs between the front and rear room, trapped between walls which could support the treads and risers and a handrail, making it cheaper to construct.

The elegant iron and wood balustrades of the Regency were not appropriate in Victorian Gothic and Revival houses so carved or turned wooden balustrades, with a newel post at the end of the flight, returned to favour. At first these may have been restricted to the first flight of stairs due to the cost, but by the middle of the century machine-made components were available bringing the cost down. Even in wooden staircases, iron may have still been used for the balustrades, in others replacing the odd wooden one to add strength to the structure, and then painted to match. The understairs area may have been boxed in and

panelled to further replicate Elizabethan and Jacobean staircases and there was a return to closed strings (where the treads run into the side panel on which the balustrades rest rather than hang over it – fig 6.10). Handrails

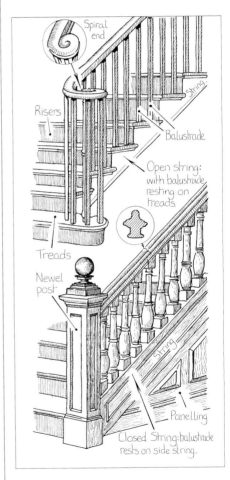

FIG 6.10: *A Regency and early Victorian open string staircase and a later revival of a 17th-century closed string staircase.*

were available in many designs, a distinctive type being the frog.

INTERIOR DOORS

Although early Victorian houses may have still used six-panelled doors, by the mid century and onwards the four-panelled door was almost universal in middle and upper class housing, comprising a frame of vertical rails and horizontal stiles, with the four panels slotted in and featuring a raised centre part (fielded), at least in the most important rooms. Cheaper versions with a flat panel and just a moulding around the edge were common while those bordering service rooms or upstairs could have a decorated side facing out and a plain inner. The panels and mouldings became generally deeper in the mid-

FIG 6.11: *The left-hand view shows the side of a four-panelled door facing the living room, the right shows the same door but without its moulding as it only faces the kitchen and is out of view of guests.*

Victorian period and in the later 19th century the longer top panels were often replaced by glass, frosted, etched or stained, usually with floral patterns. This provided extra light into the room without the loss of privacy, which was further enhanced by hinging the door so it blocked the room from view as it was opened. Many 19th-century houses have had the two ground floor rooms knocked through into one with the advent of central heating. It is sympathetic, however, to fit double doors within the dividing arch as the Victorians appreciated the convenience of being able to extend the room when entertaining and they were often fitted in large houses.

The best houses could afford the hardwoods but most had softwoods either painted or stained in imitation of them, in dark, solid colours or ebonised with a stain and black lacquer (popular in Aesthetic and Arts and Crafts interiors), although in some Arts and Crafts houses light woods like yew or ash were left unpainted. Most working-class houses and some cellars and attic rooms in better houses would often use simple batten-plank doors, vertical planks held together by horizontal or diagonal battens on the inner face. This type of door which had been used since medieval times also reappeared in some of the Domestic Revival and Arts and Crafts houses.

Hinges were hidden from view between the doorcase and door as they are today, with brass or iron butt hinges. Simple strap hinges were needed on batten-plank doors, although Arts and

FIG 6.12: *A simple batten-plank door from an attic room and a four-panelled door on the right finished in a typical dark wood effect.*

Crafts designers made a feature of these with iron, elongated and patterned types. Internal doors usually had round knobs fitted, with brass in the best but china (either white, black or with a pattern transferred on) and turned-wood being the most widely used. The knob was often used in conjunction with a brass or china fingerplate on the stile, plain in early houses but more elaborate later. Surface mounted locks were still used in Victorian houses in brass, iron and even wood casing, but the newly developed mortice lock, set within the door with just the keyhole exposed, became popular. With them came a selection of escutcheons in round, oval and tear-drop shaped metal or china, designed to protect the edge of the hole and avoid dust getting into the mechanism.

CEILINGS AND FLOORS

Although most rooms would probably have plain ceilings, many of which were white, the better examples were plastered with raised patterns which, especially in the 1850s and 1860s, could be elaborately coloured. These patterns were usually imitations of historic types, from shallow Classic and flamboyant Rococo in the early years to Elizabethan and Jacobean deep geometric designs in the 1850s and 1860s. In the later Victorian period, there was a reaction against these heavy and hard to clean ceilings, although builders still fitted ceiling roses and cornices until the turn of the century. The introduction of Anaglypta relief papers in the late 1880s made it cheaper and easier to cover ceilings. A ceiling rose was usually fitted above central chandeliers and gas lights not only as a decorative tool, but also to catch the soot rising from the

FIG 6.13: *A Victorian ceiling rose with an Anaglypta paper around it.*

flames, some even having vents built into the design which ducted outside.

For the majority of the working population of both town and country, ground floors might only have been beaten earth or a covering of cheap clay tiles. It was only in terraces with a cellar and the better quality houses of the later Victorian period that floorboards were used throughout.

Most Victorian ground floors were of boards suspended above an air gap to avoid damp, or over a cellar or basement. The boards on this and the other floors ran at right angles to the joist beneath, which in turn rested on either a ledge in the brickwork (the wall becoming thinner and thinner which each level), a timber plate fixed into the wall or, in cheaper and smaller houses, into slots created by leaving out bricks. Machine cutting introduced in the 1830s produced accurately shaped boards, wider at first but narrower later, which were usually butted up against each other with some form of

FIG 6.14: *Later narrow Victorian boards with the nail heads exposed.*

dowel between in some examples to avoid warping. Their narrow ends rested over a joist which they were nailed onto either discreetly at an angle through the cut end in the best situations or simply from above, leaving the nail head exposed. In the later 19th century mass-produced tongue and groove versions were increasingly available. Boards in the best houses and especially in the rooms where they would be on show were of polished mahogany or oak. Pine was used elsewhere, although as usual it was stained, painted, varnished or polished to look like a hardwood (it was also scrubbed with sand and limewater to give an almost white finish in rooms like the bathroom).

Parquet flooring, thin pieces of hardwood laid in patterns, was still used in some of the best houses in the early Victorian period, especially around the borders of the floor which were not covered by the central carpet. After the mid 19th-century fashion for completely carpeted floors, parquet flooring made a come-back, especially now ready-made veneered panels were available off the shelf. A new flooring which first appeared in the 1860s was linoleum, a compressed mixture of cork, sawdust, oils and glues on a canvas backing. This imitated more expensive flooring types and was popular in bedrooms, bathrooms and nurseries in middle-class housing. In the country, marbles, limestone and slate floors could be found in the finest halls while flagstones or tiles were common in service areas and farmhouses.

The most distinctive form of

FIG 6.15: *Plain red tiled floor with black border used in service rooms. The line of the border tiles can indicate where old internal walls may have been removed, especially larders in kitchens.*

Victorian flooring was the ceramic tile, plain tiles (quarries) in red and black for kitchens and service areas and patterned encaustic tiles for display, most notably in the porch and along the hall. Encaustic tiles (meaning 'burnt in') were made by stamping a design into the wet clay and filling it with a

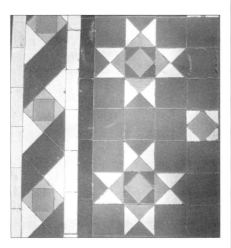

FIG 6.16: *Geometric coloured tiles pre-shaped in squares, triangles, diamonds and rectangles formed distinctive patterned floors in halls, porches and conservatories.*

different colour slip, before the firing fused them together leaving either a glazed or more typically unglazed tile. Monasteries had been the centre of their production in the medieval period, but the knowledge was lost after the Dissolution. The process was revived in the early 19th century, with at first only a basic colour range of cream, red, brown and black. As these tiles were still expensive, they were used in small numbers along with cheaper, plain six-inch square quarries or geometric tiles which came in pre-cut shapes. In the second half of the century, mass-produced versions now including colours like blue and green became affordable to the middle classes. Unglazed floor tiles were usually polished and sealed after cleaning with linseed oil and a coat of wax.

These surfaces might be covered in places by simple home-made rag rugs. By the end of the century floorcloths (canvas treated with various substances to imitate carpet) were becoming affordable. Hand-woven carpets were a luxury product (machine-made carpets became more widely available later in the century) and were reserved for the first flight of stairs and the best reception rooms, but then were rarely seen under a variety of protective coverings. These ranged from a hearth rug to druggets (a type of floorcloth), crumb cloths and newspaper which not only protected the valuable carpet but also made the arduous task of cleaning with a dustpan and brush much easier. Floorcloths imitating better quality coverings were widely used and were available in all sizes and designs.

Oriental rugs remained popular, especially with the Japanese-inspired Aesthetic movement of the 1870s.

WALLS

Internal walls were plastered in layers either directly onto the stone or brickwork or onto horizontal laths (thin strips of wood) in the case of stud walls. The finished surface was edged and divided up by various mouldings and then either painted (with a water-based paint which allowed the new plaster to dry thoroughly over the first year or so, or an oil-based paint), papered, panelled or tiled.

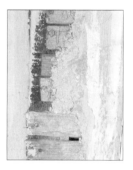

FIG 6.17: *Laths nailed onto a vertical post in a stud wall and then plastered and painted.*

Mouldings: Dado, Cornice, Picture Rail and Skirting

Another important decorative element around the Victorian house was the use of various mouldings to divide up the wall, again the most elaborate being reserved for the principal rooms. They were originally used to cover up joints which might open up after time, or to give protection to surfaces liable to damage: skirting board along the bottom, a dado or chair rail fitted three or four foot up (to protect the wall from the backs of chairs), a picture

rail (to hang pictures from) and a coving or cornice along the top (see fig 6.1). The combination of these features varied through the 19th century depending on fashion.

By the Regency and early Victorian period, the old fashion of having chairs moved up against the wall when not in use, and hence having the dado rail to protect the wall, had fallen from favour. The table had become permanently positioned in the middle of the room. Owners wanted to show off their new wallpapers so a clear wall, with the exception of perhaps a picture rail high up, was required. In the mid 19th century the cornice and skirting had grown in size, depth and elaboration to make up in some way for the lack of moulding on the wall, and the cornice even spread out horizontally across the ceiling. By the 1870s, the dado and picture rails had come back into fashion (although the former served no practical use) and combinations of both or just one or the other were usual up to the turn of the century. Their position on

FIG 6.18: *This cornice (left) which typically of mid to late Victorian styles spread out onto the ceiling, incorporates the same fluted design and Tudor rose emblem as the door surround (right) in the same room.*

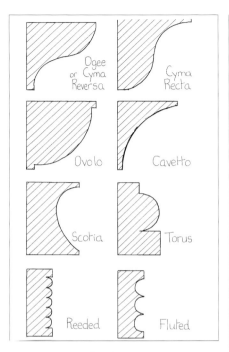

FIG 6.19: *Popular elements to Victorian mouldings (fluted and reeded were more common in Regency mouldings).*

Victorian mouldings were usually made from either plaster, especially for cornices and coving, or wood for more damage-prone areas like the skirting, picture and dado rails. By the middle of the century, elaborate designs were becoming available 'off the shelf' rather than being crafted on site. Their profiles changed through time and although some mouldings can appear complex, they have at their core some basic shapes (fig 6.19) which might have been repeated on all the mouldings within the room (fig 6.18). Some were embellished with designs which would have been appropriate to a particular room, like fruits in a dining room, or floral motifs in a drawing room, which can help to identify its original use. In Regency and early Victorian houses,

the wall could vary; in the later years the picture rail moved down to run in line with the top of the doorcase, creating a large frieze above. By the 1880s they also tended to be smaller and simpler in design, in part to make them less of a dust trap in a society which was becoming obsessed with hygiene. In general, elaborate mouldings were used in the main reception rooms, but most bedrooms in a large or medium house were still expected to have a coving and skirting boards and some of the service and servants' rooms may have had the latter.

FIG 6.20: *Examples of Victorian skirting board, cornice, picture rail and door surround.*

rather flat, reeded or fluted mouldings were popular. By the mid-Victorian period these had been replaced by bolder profiles with the ogee shape (a reverse 's' shape also known as cyma reversa) featuring in many designs, while torus (a large bead shape) was popular on the skirting right up to the end of the century. By the end of the Victorian period, Classical styles were being revived, in particular the bolection and cyma recta moulding, although the exclusive houses built by Arts and Crafts designers heralded in a new lighter style of interior, devoid of moulding.

Paints

Ready mixed paints in a tin were not introduced until the end of the 19th century. Painting remained a professional job with decorators or builders having their own paint recipes. Oil-based paints were made up from ingredients including lead and turpentine while water-based ones contained chalk and glue. Colours for most of the Victorian period came from natural products, with those from expensive minerals inevitably costing more. Despite this limitation, rooms were decorated in a wide variety of colour combinations and shades. Although there is an image of dark and gaudy coloured interiors, lighter shades were often used. However, strong colours which were especially popular in the 1850s and 1860s were also chosen for practicality, as the smoke generated by the fire, gas lights and candles within and the filth which came from outside could quickly ruin lighter schemes.

Some popular colours used for interiors included deep reds in the early years as they made an effective background for gilded picture frames in principal rooms, while lilac, brown/beige and terracotta were often used in conjunction with lighter tones and colours. In the mid-Victorian period combinations of dark colours rather than different shades of the same were used, including olive green, burgundy, browns and blue. By the 1870s these had been replaced by more muted colours with plum, rose and sage green popular. Arts and Crafts houses towards the end of the century started to use lighter colours, including creams and white (in the hygiene-conscious later years owners wanted to see the dirt to help cleaning). Whatever the period, in general, male orientated

FIG 6.21: *A detail of a window frame finished in a wood grain effect. Victorians only started using white frames when the Queen Anne style came to prominence in the 1870s.*

rooms like the dining room, library or study were painted in strong colours, while female ones like the morning or drawing room in lighter tones. Where different shades were used they became lighter higher up the wall.

Exterior details like doors and window frames were usually in dark colours early on, browns, greens and graining effects being popular, then finished off with a varnish. White painted joinery only became popular in the 1870s and 1880s with the Queen Anne-style houses.

Wallpaper

The Victorian age was a boom time for wallpaper with the repeal of all restrictions on their production and the invention of continuous rolls of paper, rotary printing machines and artificial dyes, all by the 1860s. Machine-made papers had become popular around the time Victoria came to the throne, although the patterns were limited to repeats of no more than half a foot due to the size of rollers. Many had simple geometric designs over the whole or just the background, while flock wallpapers were re-introduced in the 1850s. Other wallpapers imitated elaborate Rococo designs, featured painted scenes or commemorated famous events like battles.

Professional designers despised these, seeing them as fake, tacky and over the top. From the 1850s they introduced what they believed were more appropriate, two-dimensional patterns using floral motifs and geometric designs, many with a medieval theme for the popular Gothic revival houses of the time. These more subdued patterns avoided distracting the eye from the mass of pictures which were being hung on the wall at the time. They were produced in dark colours like green and burgundy (especially after chemical dyes made from coal tar were introduced in 1856) although lighter golden yellows, creams and beige/browns were also used. Artists like William Morris are associated with these mid and late Victorian papers but their work was actually exclusive and limited; the vast majority of papers being brought out

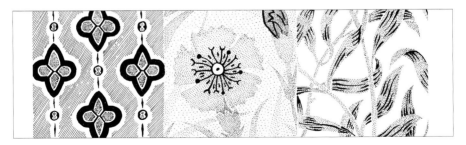

FIG 6.22: *Early papers often included simple, small geometric patterns (left) while more stylish two-dimensional floral designs were popular in the 1860s and 1870s (middle). Later papers had more highlighting creating a three-dimensional effect (right).*

FIG 6.23: *Embossed papers used on the frieze and ceiling, dating from the late Victorian period.*

FIG 6.24: *Glazed wall tiles were used to line halls, kitchens, bathrooms and, in this case, entrance porches.*

were mass produced and many were designed in imitation of their work. Later wallpapers became lighter with patterns shown in some relief with highlighting and shadows. With the re-introduction of dados and picture rails in the 1870s a selection of different sized papers, borders and friezes were produced to suit, which by this time might also be advertised as more hygienic with the removal of substances like arsenic and lead which were still being used for printing. Embossed papers appeared in the late 1870s with Lincrusta (produced by the same company who made linoleum in a similar way but using wood pulp rather than cork) and in the late 1880s with the lighter and more versatile Anaglypta. These were especially popular along the dado in the hall and stairs, for friezes, and especially Anaglypta, across ceilings.

Wall Tiles

Glazed wall tiles, usually six inches square (although hexagons and octagonal shapes were available) were popular, especially in the later 19th century when mass-produced versions spread down the social scale. They were either plain, had transfer printed patterns or an embossed design. They were available in white, as often used in kitchens, as well as a range of colours like green, turquoise and creams. Often lighter shades were favoured so that dirt would stand out to make cleaning easier. From the 1870s plain or patterned tiles were used for lining the sides and hoods of register grates. In some houses the hall had a covering up to the waist rail (about a foot higher than a dado), including floral designs and landscape views, while Arts and Crafts designers also produced their own handmade tiles.

Panelling

Panelling had generally been replaced by plaster walls with applied mouldings by the late 18th century but with the

FIG 6.25: *The scalloped pelmets recessed into the window revealed on the left are all that remain of external blinds which would have shaded the window in much the same way as the modern versions on the right.*

FIG 6.26: *A sash window catch with a ceramic knob.*

Revival movement it again became fashionable especially in the best quality houses, along halls and under stairs. Arts and Crafts designers also reintroduced wainscot, in the form of vertical boards usually running two thirds or three quarters of the way up the wall and capped at the top by a plate rail (a three to four inches wide shelf).

WINDOWS
Curtains and blinds

Curtains and blinds were not only important to maintain privacy and keep out draughts, but also to protect valuable fabrics and furniture prone to fading in sunlight. In larger houses the main windows would normally have many layers. An outer layer nearest the window was a blind; the earliest ones were often wooden slatted Venetian types, though later roller blinds with plain or patterned fabrics were popular, some even having scenes painted upon them. In the middle was a layer of lace or muslin, which was valuable for catching dirt from outside, with

possibly another chintz, velvet or damask hanging in front. The inner curtain would often be in a heavy fabric like a tapestry with a pelmet above and loops to the side as tie backs, the whole making a great display of the owner's pretensions. Further protection could be attained from outside with the addition of a bonnet blind, a colourful canvas on a roller, set within a box above the window. It could be pulled out to cast shade below. The canvases have long since rotted away but the boxes they were held in can often still be found, especially above Regency and early Victorian windows.

Shutters

Security was just as important as it is today to those who had valuables worth stealing and the best houses had internal, lockable shutters fitted. These were panelled and either folded out of cases to the side of the sash window or rose out of a box below the sill. The windows themselves would have catches on top of the lower sash, often with a pin or screw part to avoid a knife being inserted from outside, and metal sash lifts on the bottom. These were usually made from brass, sometimes with a ceramic knob on the catch, while side opening casement windows which returned to popularity with the late Victorian revivalists often had iron fittings.

LIGHTING

The inside of a Victorian house at night would seem incredibly dark to our modern eyes. Candles only gave off about a fortieth of the light produced by a modern sixty watt bulb, oil lamps around a tenth, and gas lights at best a quarter. It was therefore usual to have numerous fixed and portable light sources in one room which could be close to a person reading, working or playing. Combinations from oil lamps and candles in the early years to gas lights and oil lamps later were used together.

Candles

Despite the introduction of new gas and oil lamps, the candle remained the standard source of light for the majority of people up to the late 19th century. The best types were those made from beeswax, which as they hardly dripped were ideal for the chandeliers of the wealthy, spermaceti (until the sperm whale became virtually extinct), and then in the 1830s from synthetic fatty acids and later still paraffin wax. Tallow candles were commonly used by the middle classes and artisans and were dipped in animal fat. They produced a weak light for about two hours but were rather smelly and dirty. Worse still were the rushlights or dips, which were simply the outer leaves of rushes dipped in animal fat and clipped

into a holder, which provided at best a quarter to half an hour's light and needed constant trimming to prevent soot. Candleholders had changed little from traditional designs, although some had devices to push the candle up as it burned.

Oil Lamps

Oil lamps were another ancient form of lighting which were improved upon in the late 18th and 19th centuries, principally by increasing the air flow to the flame so it gave off more light and less smoke, and by raising the oil reservoir above the light to use gravity to increase the flow of oil to the wick. Early Victorian lamps typically used rape seed (colza), olive or palm oil but these were replaced from the 1850s by paraffin oil (distilled from coal) which being thinner could flow up to the wick without the need to suspend the holder above the light. (However, as the old lamps had been expensive purchases, many were still used long after paraffin was introduced.) Oil lamps hung from the ceiling would typically be held by a small vertical rod, with curving shaped brackets or chains hanging from it to support the reservoir and wick, while portable lamps often imitated plain or decorated candlesticks or were shaped like classical urns. Simple glass globes were often used on the latter while in the middle of the century lampshades made from fabric and decorated with showers of hanging beads were popular.

Gas Lamps

Gas lighting systems had been introduced in the 18th century and gas

FIG 6.27: *Early gas lights had the flame burning up (left), but later improved mantles gave better light shining down (right).*

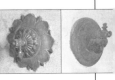

works supplying street and factory lights were common. However, its use in the home only took off in the 1850s and 1860s, especially after it had been installed in the new Houses of Parliament. Despite the fact that it burned five times brighter than most candles, it produced excessive soot and noxious gases so was limited to downstairs and struggled in popularity against the new paraffin lamps. From the 1880s new incandescent lights, which burned twice as bright, increased in popularity, as they could be turned down to reduce soot but still produce an acceptable light. By the end of the century slot meters were introduced making gas lamps accessible to the working classes.

Gas lights when hung from the ceiling

tended to imitate existing forms of fixed lights like chandeliers or oil lamps, except with a pipe coming down to the burner and often some type of pulley system to bring them closer for lighting. Wall mounted types had the gas fed through a decorated, plain, curved or swan-neck shaped pipe to the burner. Early types of these were open and fish-tail shaped. These were replaced in the late 1880s by the new incandescent burners covered by mesh mantles, which in the 1890s were turned upside down to reduce shadows in the room. Portable gas lamps were also available from the mid 19th century with long rubber hoses supplying the gas (much like a Bunsen burner), which obviously limited how far they could move. Shades were mainly of glass in a wide variety of shapes, finishes and colours reflecting the fashion of the time.

Electric Lights

Although invented and developed in the late 19th century, it was not until the beginning of the following century that electric lighting became popular, especially after the introduction of incandescent bulbs in 1907 for the few that could afford them. The bulbs would have seemed dim at first to modern eyes, yet were sufficiently bright for stained-glass shades to be popular to reduce the glare!

FIG 6.28: *Two simple late Victorian ceiling gas lights with chains to control the flow.*

CHAPTER 7

Reception and Living Rooms

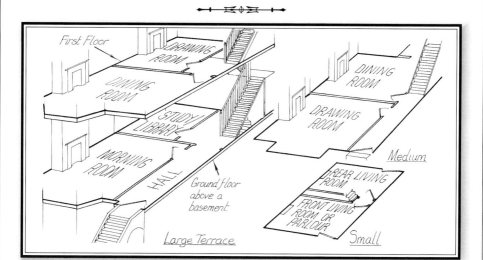

FIG 7.1: *Plans of a large (left), medium (top right) and small terrace house (bottom right) showing the possible arrangement of the living rooms.*

LARGE AND MEDIUM HOUSES

In the houses of the upper and more successful middle-class family, the principal ground or first floor rooms were intended for entertaining and impressing guests, as much as for being lived in. They would range in number from a moderate-sized front and back parlour, with a hall and service rooms at the rear, to a suite of at least four richly decorated rooms reflecting their specific roles and the sex which predominantly used them. In the early Victorian large, urban terrace the most important of these rooms in which the entertaining took place were on the first floor, the *piano noble*, with the everyday rooms used by the family on the ground floor, itself raised above the service rooms in the half basement below. In later Victorian detacheds, semis and most large terraces, these principal rooms were more likely to be on the ground floor, with the service rooms in a suite at the rear.

Hall

The first room past the front door which the visitor came upon was the hall. Its main role was to impress upon them the wealth and aspirations of the owner while they waited to be seen. Most were narrow spaces with tall ceilings, although in the larger houses, especially in the later Victorian period, wider halls were created. They had a large front door with flanking windows and sometimes an internal vestibule, with a further glass door to help keep out draughts and dirt (a curtain may have been hung over this as a further barrier).

FIG 7.2: *A later Victorian hall from a large house with room for a small table, chair, coat stand and a compact fireplace. Note the heraldic glass in the margin windows either side of the door, the geometric tiled floor and the dark coloured embossed paper on the dado.*

FIG 7.3: *Two examples of the distinctive arch at the end of the hall near the stairs, often supported on corbels (brackets) as in the top right example.*

Decoration was rich and builders usually fitted ornamental details like cornices, friezes and skirtings. The most distinctive of these were the elaborate brackets (corbels) supporting an arch, which as it was carrying the dividing wall on the floor above was in the middle of the house, towards the end of the hall near the stairs. The lower section of the wall (the dado) could be covered with wainscoting or panelling in the early years. Glazed wall tiles became popular from the 1860s and Lyncrusta or Anaglypta papers were favoured from the 1880s. Anaglypta would usually be painted and varnished in dark colours, often in imitation of marble or leather. Above the dado rail wallpapers containing dark greens, browns and burgundy were popular, the strong colours creating warmth upon entry. Although most halls were

narrow, there was usually room to squeeze in a small table for calling cards to be left upon, a couple of chairs for waiting visitors and a hat and coat stand. Wider more elaborate vestibules could even have a fireplace, pictures or portraits upon the wall and a grandfather clock, with the masculine nature of the hall further enhanced by animal heads hung on the wall and heraldic glass in the door or side windows.

The other notable feature of Victorian halls was their treatment of the floor. Early examples probably had oiled cloths or parquet flooring, but from the 1850s encaustic tiles became popular in the larger houses, with at first earthy and later more bold-coloured geometric patterns within borders. Some of the best early housing may have had marble flooring, but by the late 19th century mosaics formed out of black and white or coloured stones had become more widely popular.

FIG 7.4: *Two geometric tiled hallways from middle-class terrace houses.*

Dining Room

In all houses of this size a separate dining room reserved for special occasions and entertaining guests was required. Not only were the numerous courses of Victorian meals taken here but the gentlemen of the group would stay behind to smoke and talk after the ladies had retired. Its decoration tended to reflect this masculine use, with strong colours and large-scaled interior features. An impressive marble, stone or hardwood fireplace, a large mahogany square, rectangular or round table with upholstered chairs and a sideboard with open shelves above in which to display the best china and silver were standard fittings. In the early Victorian house, dining chairs were still put up against the wall so a dado rail was usually fitted to protect it. However, by the second half of the century the chairs were generally pushed under the table. Later in the period Arts and Crafts designers recommended simpler designed oak tables and chairs with rush matted seats.

Walls were often decorated with patterned or flock wallpapers in dark reds or green, sometimes with wooden panelling covering the dado below. These strong colours were considered an appropriate background for the pictures which would be hung from horizontal brass rods and also suited the low light given off by the candles on the table, creating a warm and intimate atmosphere. The frieze or cornice, might incorporate designs with a food theme, for example, grapevines or fruits. In the early years the floor would usually be covered by a carpet with a two to three foot border, and later by a completely fitted one,

although a separate drugget was positioned under the table to catch crumbs.

Drawing Rooms

The drawing room (shortened from the original title of withdrawing room) was most frequently occupied by the ladies. Its feminine nature was reflected in lighter, more elegant decoration with forms like swags of flowers and leaves featuring in the friezes and cornices. It was also the principal space for displaying the increasing clutter of antiques, treasures and ornaments for the admiration of guests. Unlike the more spacious dining room, it tended to become increasingly crammed with all manner of furniture including sofas, chairs, footstools, writing and games tables, display cabinets and a piano. The seating would be arranged in separate, intimate groupings around the large fireplace or smaller tables.

Early drawing rooms may have still reflected the Classical taste with flamboyant, Rococo-type friezes, patterned ceilings, gilt-finished wall panelling with inset fabrics, as well as wallpapers in lighter creams, greys, pinks and blue. Gothic style and mid-Victorian houses might have had wooden panelling or darker coloured papers in sage green, ochre, rose and earthy reds with a collection of paintings and even tapestries seemingly scattered at random upon the walls. There would always have been a prominent fireplace of marble, stone or hardwood and luxurious curtains in up to four layers with pelmets above. In later drawing rooms, handmade, embroidered wall

FIG 7.5: *A medium-sized Victorian drawing room with its close groupings of furniture, busy decoration and upright piano in the right corner.*

hangings might replace wallpaper and more hygienic exposed floorboards with hand-woven rugs were advocated, rather than a large carpet. Late 19th century houses, under the influence of Arts and Crafts designers, rejected the cluttered treasure trove altogether and used light-coloured walls and a more spacious layout.

Morning Rooms or the Parlour

In large houses there would also have been a private family room for everyday use, usually called a morning room or a parlour (from the French verb '*parler*' meaning to speak). Despite its general function it was most frequently used by ladies for pastimes like sewing and embroidery and hence there would

have been a lighter, feminine feel to the decoration.

In the medium-sized house there would be just two living rooms on the ground floor, often referred to as parlours, the front one generally reserved for guests and special occasions and the rear for everyday living, with sometimes sliding or folding doors between so they could be opened up into one. In the rear parlour, in an attempt to emulate his social superiors the owner would often fit a small corner bookcase or shelves to create the feel of a library, which was an object of desire for the middle-class gentleman at the time. The decoration of the front room might reflect that of the dining room of a large house, while the multi-purpose rear parlour would take on the appearance of a miniature drawing room but in the general style of the day.

Library

Nearly every large house had a library which acted not only as a storage room for books and manuscripts but also as a study or morning room for gentlemen. Its masculine nature was reflected in the styling of the room, with rich colours or panelling, Gothic and Elizabethan inspired features and ceilings, an imposing fireplace and leather-covered seats. The bookcases would preferably be of oak or mahogany and if not were in a softwood painted in a dark colour or stained. They were open at the top, often with period detailing and closed at the bottom with doors, to protect important manuscripts and documents. Other furniture included a desk, a lectern, a table (often leather covered) for displaying literature upon, and possibly an easel near the window as painting was a popular pastime which took place here.

Smoking and Billiards Rooms

Victorians increased the number of rooms and created corridors in their largest houses to both separate the family from the servants and accommodate an increasing number of pastimes. The most distinctive of the age which could be found in a gentleman's urban residence were the smoking and billiards rooms, preferably sited close to each other with the former having a high ceiling and the latter usually on the ground floor. The decoration was bold with walls panelled or decorated to imitate stone or leather, elaborate cornices or friezes, dark-coloured curtains, chairs covered in velvet or leather and a large, marble fireplace all being popular. The billiards room was seen as a den of iniquity and its decoration may have reflected this, with exotic Turkish or Moorish designs around the playing table with its distinctive row of hanging lights.

SMALL HOUSES

The living space for the vast majority of the urban population ranged from just a single room within an old house in which the working-class family had to both eat and sleep, to the front and rear living room which was becoming standard by the end of the century.

FIG 7.6: *A Victorian back-to-back living room (furnished in an Edwardian style) with a compact open range, cupboards fitted in the alcoves to the side of the fireplace and a central table with a few chairs out of view.*

Single Living Rooms

Perhaps due to their limited space, the lifestyle of the working-class family living in a single room within an old house or a back-to-back, differed from that of those above them in the social scale. The men of the house worked long hours and many spent the few leisure hours they had in the evening at the public house. Women also usually had a job. The children were either out playing or working and were often sent straight to bed. This limited the amount of time that the whole family (averaging around five to six) would be all together in what was usually no more than a twelve by twelve foot room. There was also little time or space for cooking so most ate 'take away' food like meat chops and pies. Anything prepared in the living room would be taken round to the local bake house, which was often just an oven in the basement of a local shop. Only simple tasks like toasting bread or heating soup took place in the home.

Furniture was limited and most had little which required storage. There would have been a cheap wooden table and a few chairs, a simple fireplace with probably a hob grate so water could be boiled on the side, and either wooden floorboards, a plain tiled or even a beaten earth floor. In the back-to-backs and similar small terraces, which were not always slums, the residents did have the scope to improve their surroundings as wages increased. Walls could be decorated with paper or cheaper stencilling, oilcloths and rag-rugs covered the floor and shelves or wall cupboards could be fitted to house what crockery and ornaments they owned. There would also need to be space to store the coal, usually in the cellar or under the stairs, while a separate cupboard was often built into the side of the chimney breast for further storage.

Front and Rear Living Rooms

For better-off working families a two-up two-down terrace, with a front and rear living room, might be affordable, especially by the end of the century. In most the front and back doors opened directly into the respective rooms, but in later examples a short or narrow hallway might be squeezed into the better houses enabling the owner to create a front parlour which could be reserved for special occasions. In houses with two living rooms, the rear would usually have taken on the appearance of a kitchen with a central scrubbed-down table, chairs and in later examples, a small cast-iron cooking range, sink and cold water tap. The front room would have been more relaxing with upholstered chairs, rugs or floor cloths, decorated walls and a modest fireplace with a register grate.

FIG 7.7: A *front (top) and rear (bottom) living room from a two-up two-down terrace.*

CHAPTER 8

Service Rooms

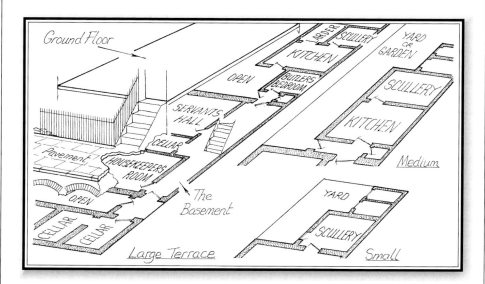

FIG 8.1: *Possible layouts of service rooms in the basement and rear extension of a large terraced house (left) and the rear extensions of a medium (top right) and small terrace (bottom right).*

The service area in a Victorian house could range from whole suites of specialist rooms in the largest houses, which would be in the basement in the earlier examples and in rear extensions later on, down to just a kitchen and scullery in many middle-class homes. With the introduction in the late 18th century of affordable bell systems for summoning servants and the creation of corridors and rear stairs, the service rooms could be positioned in a separate block, enabling servants to come and go out of sight of the family and guests. This segregation was further enhanced in larger houses with the covering of the ground floor door into the service area with a green baize padding to reduce noise from the kitchen. The stud holes on the rear side which held it in place can sometimes still be found.

The working classes had little need for separate service and storage rooms. For most of the period they tended to eat few vegetables, fruit only in the form of jam, were suspicious of milk (with good reason as much of it contained chemicals to enhance its shelf life) and really only aspired to eating meat which was generally cooked elsewhere. What domestic work there was took place in the rear living room, although in the better examples and many later homes there would have been a scullery and perhaps a larder.

Kitchens

The kitchen was the principal service room where most of the preparation and cooking of meals took place, although not the washing up. Kitchens rarely had a sink before 1900. If the architect had control of the orientation, then he would place the kitchen on the cooler north or east side, but in most terraces this wasn't possible and it was usually in the basement or at the rear. Ensuring good ventilation and lighting was important when considering the kitchen's position and design. The interior had to be fitted out with washable furniture and the walls decorated with hygienic coverings.

The range of specialist rooms, equipment and utensils tended to

FIG 8.2: *A Victorian kitchen from a large house. Most cooking was done on the range (A). This had an oven each side and hot plates above, although with the central fire exposed a freestanding roasting spit (E) could be stood in front and a warming trolley (D), which not only heated plates inside but also protected the cook from the heat. An open dresser (B) stored cooking vessels and utensils and there was a central table (C) with duck boards for standing upon below it. Other items which may be found include a knife polisher (F), a bain marie (G) for gently warming sauces, a plate rack (H) and oil lamps (I).*

increase through the period as a wider range of food became available. This was especially true in the later 19th century. Products like fish and milk could now be transported quickly, cheaper imported meat and corn became available and the resulting agriculturally depressed cereal growing areas in the South and East turned to market gardening, producing a wider range of fruit and vegetables. This enabled the growing middle classes to start creating the kinds of meals which only their social superiors had been able to eat in the past.

The large Victorian kitchen would always have a solid, rectangular central table for the preparation of meals. It was usually made from a softwood which could be scrubbed down with sand, soda and water, never soap, in order not to taint the food. Over time this cleaning regime would leave the hard parts of the grain standing proud above the softer, a distinctive feature of genuine kitchen furniture. Slatted wooden boards would have covered the floor on either side for the staff to stand upon, with the main surface beneath usually covered by stone slabs or tiles. The lower sections of the wall were covered in a hygienic surface, usually glazed white tiles or bricks but sometimes gloss-painted vertical boards. The upper parts of the walls were whitewashed and, especially in mid-Victorian kitchens, decorated with inspiring scripts like 'waste not want not'! There would be at least one dresser up against a wall which contained cooking equipment, utensils and some dinnerware. Although in the

best houses they were designed by the architect and could be of oak or simulated to look so, most were softwood with some painted and

FIG 8.3: *A large Victorian kitchen range (top) with ovens both sides of a closed fire, and a later smaller version with only a single oven to the left and an open fire.*

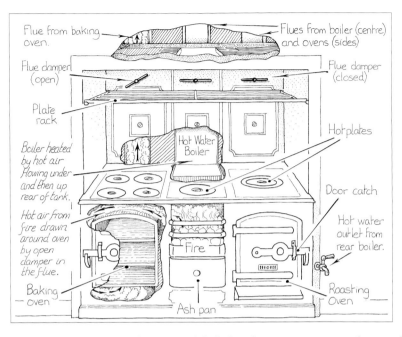

Flue from baking oven.

Flues from boiler (centre) and ovens (sides)

Flue damper (open)

Flue damper (closed)

Plate rack

Hot plates

Boiler heated by hot air flowing under and then up rear of tank.

Hot Water Boiler

Hot air from fire drawn around oven by open damper in the flue.

Door catch

Hot water outlet from rear boiler.

Fire

Baking oven

Roasting Oven

Ash pan

FIG 8.4: *A cast-iron range with its parts labelled and cut away sections showing how the heat was transferred around the ovens and up the flues at the rear.*

others scrubbed white by a similar cleaning regime to the table. The upper half, the dresser back, was usually open up to a height of seven foot, with shelves displaying the *batterie de cuisine* and everyday crockery and hooks to hold cups and jugs. Beneath this were drawers for the utensils and linen and at the bottom either an open shelf or cupboard doors to hold the larger pieces of equipment.

The most important piece of equipment in the Victorian kitchen was the cast-iron range, a combination of ovens, boiler and hobs around a central coal fire, which was built into the fireplace. The largest kitchens might even have had two of these ranges. They had developed from simple iron cradles with adjustable sides (cheeks), which appeared in the late 1600s. By the turn of the 19th century an oven and boiler were added to each side, with hobs above. These 'open' ranges, however, were deemed uneconomical and dirty so although they appeared throughout the Victorian period, it was the revised version with an enclosed fire which became popular from the 1830s, especially those manufactured by Flavels of Leamington, with the name of the town becoming synonymous with their kitcheners. These 'closed' ranges had a more compact fire enclosed beneath an iron plate which could be used for gentle heating. Flues controlled by dampers directed the hot fumes around the ovens to the side, to the boiler at the rear and then up the chimney. It was a sealed system with the old fireplace opening closed up. The sides and rear of the opening would either be tiled or covered in iron plates to match the range, with controls for the dampers and a plate-warming rack or cupboard above this.

Closed ranges reduced the amount of coal used, were much cleaner than open fires and could be left lit overnight. However, the loss of the exposed fire meant that roasting had to be done in one of the ovens, which was specially fitted with a ventilation grill to create an air flow which made the joint dry out and brown. This was not a popular arrangement and many large kitchens retained a separate traditional open fire with roasting spits and a screen or warming trolley, to reflect the heat back and give vague protection to those in the room. In response to this, range manufacturers in the later 19th century made the plates covering the fire removable so the closed range could be converted to an open type and freestanding roasters placed in front of the exposed flames (see fig 8.2). This also reduced the intense draw which small openings could create, causing coal to be consumed too rapidly and damage to parts of the range.

The adoption of cooking ranges was varied as many focused on the disadvantages, like excessive cooking smells as the old flue had been closed off, the extra cleaning they required and the fact that they could be tricky to control. They proved popular in areas associated with metal work and the coal industry, like the Midlands and the North, before being accepted nationwide. There was an element of regionalisation in the types produced, most notably in the distinctive, compact ranges of Yorkshire where the oven was raised up to one side.

The working classes rarely had ranges in the early years, with any boiling or cooking done over an open grate. They were slowly adopted in the later 19th century, although at first only in the better houses built by benevolent landlords. The types used were compact and often had a simplified design, with a sham panel to one side (especially in areas of hard water where a boiler would have been quickly

FIG 8.5: *A portable roasting spit (left) with a clockwork turning mechanism hanging in the centre (it is sited at the top when in use) and a rotary knife polisher (right).*

rendered useless). Gas-fired ranges and freestanding cookers were also slow to be accepted and did not become popular until the turn of the 20th century.

In the smaller kitchens of the middle classes, the same principal components could be found, but in a more compact form with the dresser or cupboards often fitted in the alcoves either side of the fireplace. As the staff would usually take their meals in the kitchen with this size of house, the floor might be wood boarding rather than solid so as to cut down on the noise of scraping chairs!

Sculleries

The word 'scullery' is derived from the French word for 'dish', which in turn comes from the Latin word *salver*, hence it was where the plates and dishes were washed up. The room was versatile and was used for other messy tasks like peeling vegetables, preparing meat, gutting fish or trimming candlewicks. Larger houses tended to

FIG 8.7: *Laundry equipment from a late Victorian scullery.*

have a separate laundry, but in most middle-class houses both clothes and crockery would be washed here. Due to access to piped water and drainage, the scullery was usually at the rear of the basement, in the back extension or in a separate outbuilding. It often had a tiled or flagged floor with a further drain in the middle.

Inside there would have been at least one sink, usually under the window to give the best light for cleaning. The sink could have been made from stone (if so, usually shallow), wood (which was useful for cleaning delicate china to save chipping it) or lined with soft metal sheeting, fireclay or glazed ceramic. Ceramic sinks were widely available in the second half of the century and are

FIG 8.6: *A glazed ceramic shallow sink and pump with a hot water copper in the corner behind.*

referred to today as butler or Belfast sinks. There would either be a cold water tap or a metal pump next to the sink. Hot water would be brought in from the kitchen range or sometimes from a compact version of a range in the scullery itself. Another source of hot water was the copper. This was a round metal tank with a lid, set into a brick or stone boxing (usually in a corner) and heated from below by a fire, (with separate ones for washing and heating water in larger houses).

If there was a separate laundry room, you would expect to find a copper and possibly a small range which could also be used for heating irons, a mangle (wooden rollers at first but rubber in the last decades of the 19th century), a table or bench, and drying racks suspended from the ceiling. In small houses the scullery (often referred to as the wash room or wash house) was used for all washing tasks, with even the tin bath hung up here or built in below a trap door in the floor, which could be lifted on bath night. In back-to-backs and some other small terraces, the scullery was usually a separate block at the rear, in a courtyard or at the end of a row and was shared between a number of families.

Larders, the Pantry, and Refrigeration

Food storage always posed a problem in the days before fridges and freezers. Even in the smaller houses there would have been a larder (from the Latin *lardum* meaning bacon), or pantry. 'Pantry' is the term originally given to the room where bread was stored (the

FIG 8.8: *An ice box found in larger houses usually for storage of perishables like fish. Ice was placed into the compartment to the side which cooled the lead-lined interior.*

Latin for which is *panis*). However, by the Victorian period it was also used for storing dairy products and some meats, and is often referred to as the dry larder. These rooms were preferably positioned on the north or east side, but even if they were in the sun, careful shading of the exterior wall by an overhanging roof or foliage and keeping the door shut inside could maintain a cool temperature. Stone or tiled floors, whitewashed walls and a small window covered by a perforated metal sheet or gauze helped to keep them dry. Solid slate or marble shelves at waist height provided a cool surface for dairy products and setting jellies and cream, while the remainder of food stuffs were stored on painted wooden shelves, with metal hooks in the ceiling for hanging meat. Although many larders have since been knocked out in order to fit in a modern kitchen with all its appliances, they can often be identified by the distinctive small windows and their outline from the border tiles in the original flooring.

Surprisingly, there were some forms of refrigeration in the Victorian period, one type being an ice cupboard, which had a lined interior and a chamber to the side into which ice was poured, and was used to keep dishes and products cool (see fig 8.8). Urban houses had to get their ice delivered by a merchant or fishmonger, who would travel round in the early years with Norwegian or American imports. By the second half of the century ice was produced by commercial machines in the local area. They would simply hack a piece off which was then put directly into the ice cupboard or into a churn used to make the popular ice cream. Natural ice was never put directly into drinks.

Servants' Hall, Housekeeper's and Butler's Room

In the largest urban and country houses, the hierarchy of servants demanded

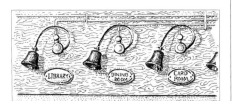

FIG 8.9: *Bell pulls were fitted in larger houses, operated by wires running through pipes in the walls.*

FIG 8.10: *The front door bell was activated by pulling on the metal knob, which was connected to a rod and wire leading to the bell in the house.*

additional rooms, in particular for the housekeeper and butler. The housekeeper's room was usually positioned where she could keep an eye on the comings and goings of staff, typically in the basement near the front and close to the servants' hall. In here she may have kept the china, general crockery and table linen as well as her own office furniture, a chair, fireplace and bed. The butler's pantry or bedroom would be similarly fitted out and could also store some crockery, cutlery and a few of the more precious pieces in a safe. As he was in charge of serving food and waiting on the owners, his room was usually at the rear, close to the back stairs and near the kitchen and drinks store. Outside his room would be the bell board with its row of sprung bells and name tags; cables running through tubes in the wall connected it to the pulls in each room, and to the metal pull rod at the front door. These complex arrangements had to be regularly oiled and tightened, a job usually done by a plumber or chimney sweep as they were used to dealing with hidden pipes.

In medium-sized houses, staff ate in the kitchen but in the largest houses a separate servants' hall or common room was provided, usually with a long table for meals although the senior servants would usually retire to their own rooms once they had finished.

CHAPTER 9

Bedrooms and Bathrooms

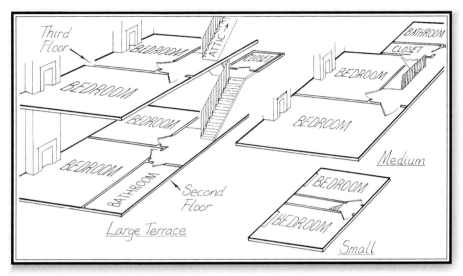

FIG 9.1: *Possible arrangement of upper floor rooms in a large (left), medium (top right) and small (lower right) terraced house.*

The upper floors in most Victorian houses were divided into bedrooms. Larger houses also had room for further divisions, with principal bedrooms having an adjoining dressing room for the gentleman and a boudoir for the lady. Boudoir comes from the French word *bouder* meaning 'to sulk' and was a place where the lady of the house could sit and sew or read. They were often sited in the rear extension, with a lower ceiling. The attic or south-facing top floor rooms,

well lit by sunlight, could be used as nurseries. They were typically decorated with wallpaper designs featuring children's tales and floored with hygienic linoleum covered by rugs. It was only later in the 19th century that bathrooms appeared.

Bedrooms

Away from the inquisitive eyes of guests, the bedroom could be a less opulent and more relaxed, personal reflection of the owner's tastes. It

FIG 9.2: *A view of the corner of a middle-class bedroom with a small fireplace, chair, wash basin, and dresser set into the bay window and a metal-framed bed in the foreground.*

tended to have a feminine leaning and was lighter and more spacious than downstairs, with pale-coloured painted walls. Later in the period, papers with, for instance, floral designs became fashionable. In the largest houses the desire for privacy extended to the married couple having separate bedrooms, albeit with a connecting door. Further down the social scale the same division was made with husbands and wives having twin beds, especially in the second half of the century. Double beds did not become common again until after the Second World War. It became increasingly important to the Victorians to have girls and boys sleeping in separate bedrooms, at first only in the largest houses but later in those of the middle classes. In existing houses an obsolete dressing room or boudoir could have been converted.

Any live-in servants would usually have their sleeping quarters in the attic, or occasionally in a small room in a rear extension.

Early Victorian beds reflected previous styles, with the old four-poster bed and the half tester with a short canopy above still being popular, with drapes hanging down from both. Although the half tester was still common in the best houses, albeit with a shorter canopy, the plain metal-framed bed, especially in brass, became standard from the 1850s. Curtains around the bed were now seen as a dirt trap. Bedrooms in large to medium houses would also have had a dressing table, covered with a cloth and often set into a bay window for the best light. Wardrobes could range from an elegant winged hardwood piece with two doors and a central mirror, to a rail in an alcove with a curtain across the front. A washstand consisting of a white basin standing on top or set into a wooden cupboard with a tiled top was often fitted into an alcove or corner. This was common in the days before the bathroom, when even the bath was taken in the bedroom in front of the fire. Most baths were filled by jugs of hot water brought up by a maid but later ones which still might be fitted even when a bathroom had been built, could have taps. Other furniture might include a chest of drawers, a small table and chair for writing and a simple fireplace in wood or cast-iron, the latter especially in lesser bedrooms and usually painted white. In the days before inside toilets, a chamber pot was kept either in the bedroom or a closet. Outside the bedrooms there may have been a housemaid's sink for washing the chamber pots out each morning.

Bedrooms in working-class terraces and back-to-backs had no such luxuries. In the early Victorian period, the whole family would often have to share the same room, or at best put the children in the attic. The situation did not improve until two-bedroom houses came within their reach in the second half of the century. Beds might be simple metal frames, with a basic feather-filled mattress. There would have been one for the parents, with the children possibly sharing four to a bed, with each child in a corner. Furniture was limited. If there was a fireplace, it was only lit when someone was sick or in labour. Floorboards were exposed with just the odd rag rug or floorcloth, while under the bed there would have been an old tin chamber pot.

FIG 9.3: *Two bedroom sets from working-class houses at the Black Country Museum. Note the washing set on the table in the right of the bottom picture and the chamber pot below the bed in the top view.*

Bathrooms

The bathroom was non-existent in early Victorian homes. Most washing was performed in the bedroom in medium or large houses, or in the rear living room or scullery in working-class homes. It was not until

FIG 9.4: *The left-hand bathroom shows how an early type from the 1860s or 1870s may have appeared with bath and basin boxed in wooden panelling. The right-hand view shows a later version with a more hygienic arrangement with open bath and basin, exposed pipework and ceramic tiled dado.*

improvements in water supply and drainage in the 1860s (with the use of cast-iron rather than lead pipes) that the first small bathrooms began to be built into new houses. They did not become a standard feature in most middle and many upper-class homes until the 1880s. While bathrooms were enthusiastically embraced by the middle classes, they were greeted with wariness by the upper classes who were still happy to let servants bring them hot water by hand.

The first bathrooms, like many new technologies, were wrapped in a familiar, non-threatening cloak. The new pressed metal baths, ceramic wash basins (known as a lavatory) and their pipework were set in mahogany cupboards and boxing. The rooms often had a fireplace, chair, small table, pictures, rugs, cornices and patterned wallpaper (especially when bathrooms were fitted into existing houses, when they were formed from a bedroom or dressing room). The bath itself was usually painted on the inside in a plain off-white or marble effect early on, with white enamelled finishes becoming common in the 1870s.

Changes came to the bathroom in the following decade as the drive for improved hygiene saw the introduction of white glazed ceramic sanitary ware. The wooden boxing was ripped out to leave all elements, especially the pipework, exposed. This move was partly due to the Prince of Wales' near fatal bout of typhoid which was blamed on bad plumbing.

Walls were tiled up to the dado, freestanding roll-topped baths stood on clawed or ball feet with painted and stencilled exteriors, and wash basins were supported on painted metal wall brackets. This enabled the floor, which was now tiled or covered in linoleum, to be cleaned thoroughly. A few may have even had a shower. These ranged from existing crude appliances supplied from a simple cistern above, to the latest elaborate spray systems massed with controls offering hot and cold piped water over virtually any part of the body. The hot water supply could come from a piped supply in an insulated tank above, which in turn was topped up directly from the boiler on the kitchen range, or from a gas-fired geyser. This was a freestanding water heater, popular in the 1870s and 1880s.

In what was now a plain, sanitary room, decoration was concentrated on the fittings rather than fixtures. Pipes and taps were in brass or copper, windows could be filled with stained-glass patterns rather than blinds or curtains and details like light fittings and bathroom accessories could be elaborately decorated. Bands of coloured or patterned tiles were used on the wall with a moulded ceramic dado rail and above this either gloss paints or varnished paper, although in the finest examples tiles were used all over. For those who could not afford all this, a linoleum floor with a painted and varnished relief wallpaper was an alternative.

Indoor Toilets

For the vast majority of people, a chamber pot under the bed or in a nearby cupboard was the main way of relieving one's self inside the house, with the fortunate few having an adjoining closet with a close stool (a chamber pot with a lid and seat) or commode. These metal or ceramic containers were emptied into open sewers in the street, a cesspit under the house or into a midden (rubbish pit) at the rear, although if mixed with ashes the contents could be collected by the night soil men and sold on as fertiliser!

Earth closets were a seated box with a chamber below into which a mix of either fine soil, ash or sawdust was

FIG 9.5: *A diagram of an earth closet with a cut away section showing the hopper at the rear and bucket beneath. The earth mix would either fall into the bowl as the user stood up (as in this example) or could be operated by a lever at the front or side of the unit.*

poured after each use. They were popular from the 1850s right up to the Second World War. They were found either in an outside privy or fitted inside Victorian houses, usually in a tiny room or the space under the stairs.

Again it was the improvement of water supply, drainage (especially with new earthenware pipework and traps which prevented smells backing up from the main sewers) and the expanding urban sewerage system in the 1870s which permitted the wider introduction of water closets. Various types had been around since the late 18th century, but these early versions with funnel-shaped hoppers and separate containers below were rather complicated, prone to leaking and often had an ineffective flush.

It was not until the drive for hygiene in the later Victorian period that a new single piece, ceramic pedestal with a washdown system supplied from a new syphonic cistern (in effect, the modern toilet) first appeared. They were usually in a small separate room next to the bathroom or at least on an outside wall (especially after new regulations about ventilation came into force in 1875) in order to have access to the soil pipe. They either had a low-mounted cistern or by the turn of the century a high-mounted type activated by a brass pull chain with a ceramic or turned wood pendant. In general the family had toilet seats made from a polished hardwood while the servants and poorer families had to make do with one made from plain softwood. Modern toilet tissue was not introduced until the 1930s so pieces of newspaper or something similar would be close at hand! Although the water closet became a standard feature in most new middle and upper-class houses by the end of the Victorian period, the mass of the population were still using outside privies, which are covered in the following chapter.

CHAPTER 10

Gardens and Outbuildings

❧ ⚌◆⚏ ❧

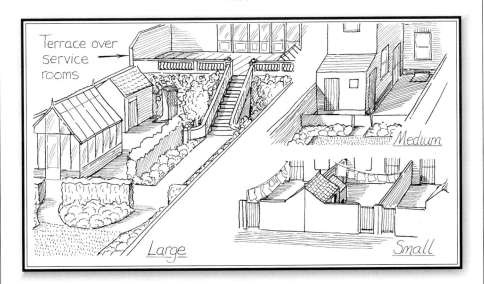

FIG 10.1: *Possible arrangements of the rears of later Victorian houses with a large (left), a medium (top right) and a small (bottom right) terraced house.*

Such was the demand for land in urban areas that houses were crammed into tight blocks with limited outdoor space. Only the largest houses were likely to have gardens and these were usually communal strips at the front and later more private areas at the rear. Typically, the larger houses fronted the road with just the well to access the basement between it and the pavement, with service buildings and possibly mews at the back. Medium houses had less still, a yard dominated by the rear extension, privy and ash bins was typical, with smaller terraces and back-to-backs at best sharing a courtyard, but often having no open space other than the narrow road in front.

In suburban and rural districts there was less pressure on land and new semis and detached houses had spacious gardens and usually a high wall or railing to maintain privacy. Part of the attraction for the middle classes of a move to the suburbs in the second half of the century was the space that was available, with a small front plot and rear garden, although there was still the scullery and privy directly behind the house. However, towards the end of the period even small two-up two-downs in industrial areas were likely to have some rear space. This might have been perhaps a yard with a small plot for growing potatoes or a communal allotment on a nearby piece of land.

Front Gardens

If there was space for a front garden in a middle or upper-class terrace it was usually small with its most notable feature being the wall or railings which enclosed it to create a measure of privacy. Railings had previously been made from wrought iron, which could be worked into wonderfully decorative patterns but was expensive, although the reduced price of iron in the 1820s meant that they could now be larger and less delicate. It wasn't until the 1850s that mass-produced cast-iron versions became widely available. They comprised vertical rails held in place at the top by a horizontal bar and at the bottom set into holes filled with lead, either in a stone base or a low wall. The finials on top could range from simple arrowheads to classical motifs while foliage designs were popular on later examples. Although most are black today, originally they would have been coloured. Early railings were painted to imitate antique metalwork, with greens and browns always popular along with dark red and blue later on.

Railings fell from favour in the 1870s on the new Queen Anne-style houses. Architects disliked the cast-iron versions which imitated wrought iron, opting for low brick walls with white painted fences on top and timber gates instead, a choice which became widespread by the turn of the century. As few houses by this time were built with basements, there was less call for railings as a safety feature along the edge of the front walls, and widely spaced decorative versions on low walls were sufficient. Many railings were ripped out in the Second World War as part of the drive to salvage metal for the war effort (although they were never really suitable for recycling). Sadly, the lead-filled sockets are often all that remain today.

Another feature found near the front door was the foot scraper. Although

FIG 10.2: *Railings from an early Victorian house (left) with finials and a top horizontal rail. On the right is the type of white fence mounted upon a low red-brick wall, which found favour in later Victorian houses.*

these were commonly found in the towns and cities it was in the new suburbs where they were essential. In the days before district councils the new roads and paths were usually left unsurfaced, and quickly became a quagmire when the rain came.

Rear Gardens

Although those living in rural areas or on the edge of towns and cities may have always had land attached to their houses, it was rare in urban areas to have much more than a yard with service areas at the back and a communal garden at the front. From

FIG 10.3: *A small walled area for growing vegetables at the rear of a late Victorian terrace, at the Black Country Museum.*

the 1850s, however, there was a growing demand for a more private space at the rear, especially for larger houses. At this time, terraces were still being built up from the ground level which meant that the garden at the back on the level of the original land had to be accessed via steps. These were typically created from a form of back terrace, sometimes with a lean-to glass house covering part of it. As in their rooms, Victorians seemed to love to cram all manner of objects into their gardens. Statues, sundials, pots, benches and a conservatory could be present, although by the late 19th century a more naturalistic approach was taken to the design and materials of these fittings and the layout with borders alongside spacious lawns and winding paths became popular.

Those in middle-class suburban houses sought to imitate their social superiors with more compact, simple versions of these gardens, still with a service area next to the house and a lawn with borders beyond. In order to distinguish themselves from the working masses, they rarely had a space for vegetables, which they could happily buy locally.

Although gardens were a rarity for most of the population, reforms meant that an increasing number towards the end of the century had access to some land for cultivation. However, the majority made do with a yard with a privy and ash bin, with only the small terraces away from the centres like railway workers' cottages having a narrow garden for growing vegetables or keeping livestock and fowl.

Conservatories

Once the reserve of the rich, new materials, techniques and mass production brought the glass house within reach of a wider population. The popularity of conservatories and greenhouses in the Victorian period was partly due to the invention of the Wardian case, a portable glass box, which for the first time permitted exotic plant specimens from around the world to be brought back and grown at home. Leading designers like Joseph Paxton and J.C. Loudon built new glass houses for these fashionable plants with domed, arched and ridge and furrow roof arrangements intended to catch the sunlight at as near to ninety degrees as possible, which was believed to be important for optimum absorption. The improvement of cast-iron, larger panes of glass and new heating systems, all made the conservatory and greenhouse a distinctive feature of especially mid to late Victorian gardens.

Conservatories were seen as an extension of the house rather than a garden feature. They were usually an annexe to a drawing room or library, with little or no connection to the garden beyond. Although they differed in material from the main structure, where possible they would be designed to complement the asymmetrical layout of the house. They could range from simple lean-to structures, often found on the rear of terraces, to complex arrangements of gables, bays, porches, domes and lanterns, with elaborate iron brackets and columns. Although the metal frame enabled these new forms to be built, it is likely that the majority of glass houses were built of wood (as long as they were not heated). They were a place for chat and snacks. Between the exotic foliage would have been cane, wicker or iron tables and chairs, tiled floors, freestanding burners or heating pipes and a fountain to provide humidity. As with all exterior wood and metalwork they were usually painted in greens and browns with the familiar white frame only becoming popular in the 1870s.

Mews

Just as the garage or drive is essential to a modern house, so the stable and yard was to the wealthy Victorian gentleman who had at least one horse and a carriage to look after. In the limited space of the large urban terrace this was done in a row of usually two-storey buildings called a mews which stood

FIG 10.4: *A row of mews now converted to housing with the main houses they were built to serve high up behind them.*

along a back lane at the rear of the property. There was a stable and storage for a carriage on the ground floor and room above for the staff. Although many of these buildings still stand today they have usually been converted into homes or garages.

Outdoor Privies

The privy (from privy chamber which meant a private room) at the rear of the house or garden was the place most people used to relieve themselves. They were typically tall, thin brick structures leaning up against the rear extension of the urban terrace, under little pitched roofs when freestanding or in rows along the ends, rears or courtyards of

FIG 10.5: *An outside privy at the end of the garden path.*

FIG 10.6: *Two examples of outdoor privies, the top showing the bucket beneath and the bottom the seat. Note on the latter the cut pieces of newspaper hanging from a piece of string on the left.*

working class houses. Most contained a simple wooden seat with a hole and a pail below, the contents of which could be poured into a cess pit or midden to be taken away by the night soil men. From the mid 19th century earth closets became widely available for both inside the house and in the privy (see fig 9.5) and remained a common sight well into the 20th century. Water closets were fitted in some later Victorian privies, especially after the 1875 Health Act and the expansion of the urban sewerage system. They typically had a high mounted cast-iron cistern and an unstained wooden seat on the ceramic bowl below. Toilet paper was a luxury which only began to appear in a roll by the 1880s and not in its modern form until the 1930s. Most people used newspaper, cut up into squares and hung from a piece of string!

Coal Cellars and Ash Bins

The most important fuel for the Victorian house was coal. Storage had to be provided for it and in large terraces with a basement the common solution was to have a coal cellar below the pavement at the front. This was a narrow brick vaulted chamber with a hole above covered by a lockable plate through which the delivery men could pour the coal, with the staff accessing it from the basement for the kitchen range and fireplaces around the house. In other houses there might be a cellar, a room which couldn't be used for anything other than storage but provided an extra barrier against rising damp. Usually there would be a trap door and some form of chute for the coal merchant to pour it down, although in small houses and back-to-backs with little access it was probably carried down. Where there was no underground space it could be kept under the stairs or in an outbuilding or coal bin in the yard.

The ashes created by the fires, even for a single house, could run into many tons a year. Ash was usually stored in a bin or outbuilding at the rear, although a communal one may have been provided, especially in back-to-backs where access for collection was so limited.

FIG 10.7: *Three examples of locking plates set in the pavement above the coal cellar. The left spiral example dates from the early Victorian period, the other two are later.*

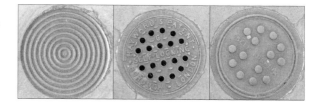

SECTION III

QUICK
REFERENCE
GUIDE

DATING HOUSES

Dating a house can be achieved visually and with documentation, the former a quick way of giving an approximate time-frame, while documentation can be time consuming but potentially more accurate. In most cases it will only be through a combination of a number of datable features and a selection of facts from various documents that the date of construction can be found. This task is much easier for Victorian houses as fashions can be pinpointed to certain decades with more accuracy and there are a greater number of records, including the first detailed maps.

Datestones: You may be fortunate enough to simply have a date emblazoned on the exterior of your house. These are usually in the form of a plaque, often with a house name, and were particularly common on middle-class housing in the second half of the century. Be wary though of a few, especially on details like gutters, as they may date from an external make-over of an older house (this is rare in the Victorian period but often happened in the previous centuries).

Visual Dating: The following timechart, showing the style of external details which were popular in approximate time-frames, and the photographs at the ends of chapters two to five will help you to identify the decades in which your house was likely to have been built. Look at the pitch of the roof, the style of original windows and doors, the bonding and uniformity of the brick, the position and prominence of the chimney, the presence and size of a rear extension

and the form of details like porches, arches and ornamentation. Caution needs to be applied though, as fashions reached different areas at different times. Although it was assumed in the past that styles originated in London and spread out across the country over the following decades, actually the coming of the railways and publishing of architectural magazines meant new ideas could travel quickly and to distant parts in a seemingly haphazard manner. For instance, at Leek in the 1870s, local builders were erecting houses in a style which you could have found in major cities some twenty years earlier. Yet at the same time, due to the town's contacts with leading figures like William Morris, architects from outside the area designed houses in a Domestic Revival style some ten years before they were common in London. So although it can be easy to identify a style, it requires looking at similar buildings in the local area and documentary evidence to establish a more precise date.

Documentary Evidence: There are numerous sources listed below, most of which are available from your local or county library or the Internet:

Maps: Ordnance Survey large-scale maps were first published from 1888-93. The small scale (one inch to a mile) first editions from 1805-73 (republished by David and Charles) could be inaccurate; second series/editions were better, begun in the 1840s and complete by the end of the century. They are a quick and easy way to see when your house appears, but be careful when interpreting the date on the map as there were revisions to add new railways and roads and it is important to check any accompanying notes for the sheet you are using. Also, they are only telling you that it was there by the time of the survey and not when it was actually built.

Trade directories: Listings of local businesses can be useful in dating when a street or row was in existence.

Victoria County Histories: A detailed series of books which after a century are still only half complete! If your town or village is covered, it is packed with useful information and often tells you when a road was laid out. Also look for *The Buildings of England* series by Nikolaus Pevsner which covers each county.

Other Sources: If you have access to your deeds they may simply answer the question, if not it might be possible to find out who the landlord was – often a company, university or landed estate – and their records, estate papers and building accounts can be useful. Local census returns, tithe surveys (late 1830s), plans for new roads and railways, fire insurance records and local papers can all be found at your county record office.

BIBLIOGRAPHY

Brunskill, R W, *Brick Building In Britain.* Victor Gollancz, 1990
Brunskill, R W, *Houses And Cottages Of Britain.* Weidenfeld Nicolson, 1997
Currer Briggs, Noel, *Debrett's Guide To Your House* (no longer in print)
Dowdy, Mac; Miller, Judith & Austin, David, *Be Your Own House Detective.* BBC Books, 1997
Eveleigh, David J, *Firegrates And Kitchen Ranges.* Shire, 2000
Hall, Linda, *Down The Garden Path: Privies In And Around Bristol And Bath.* Countryside Books, 2001
Isoabelle Ariscombe. *Arts And Crafts Style.* 1991 (no longer in print)
Lawrence, Richard Russell & Chris, Teresa, *The Period House: Style, Detail, And Decoration 1774-1914.* Weidenfeld Nicolson, 1998
McCord, Norman, *British History 1815-1906.* Oxford University Press
Miller, Judith, *Period Fireplaces.* Mitchell Beazley, 1996
Osband, Linda, *Victorian Gothic House Style.* David & Charles, 2003
Osband, Linda, *Victorian House Style.* David & Charles, 2001
Pevsner, Nikolaus, *The Buildings Of England.* Penguin (various counties and dates)
Rivers, Tony; Cruickshank, Dan; Darley, Gillian & Pawley, Martin. *The Name Of The Room,* BBC Books, 1992
Strong, Roy, *The Spirit Of Britain.* Pimlico, 2000
Taylor, Christopher, *Village And Farmstead.* George Philip, 1993
Webb, Kit, *The Victorian House (The Victorian Society Book of).* Aurum Press Ltd, 2002

TIMECHART

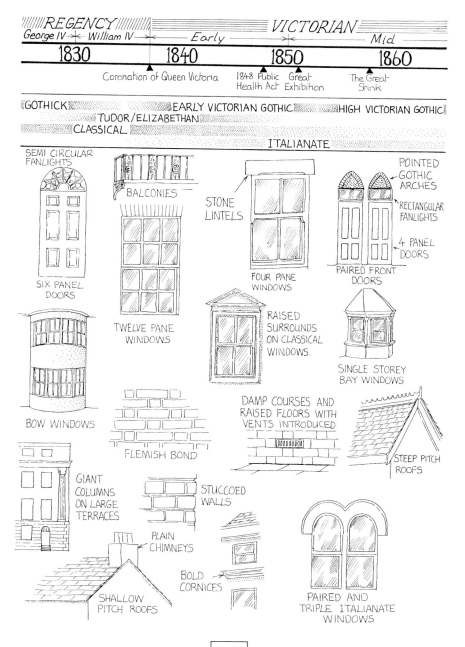

REGENCY

George IV → ← William IV → ← Early

VICTORIAN

Mid

1830   1840   1850   1860

Coronation of Queen Victoria   1848 Public Great   The Great
Health Act Exhibition   Shink

GOTHICK   EARLY VICTORIAN GOTHIC   HIGH VICTORIAN GOTHIC

TUDOR/ELIZABETHAN

CLASSICAL

ITALIANATE

SEMI CIRCULAR FANLIGHTS

BALCONIES

STONE LINTELS

POINTED GOTHIC ARCHES

RECTANGULAR FANLIGHTS

4 PANEL DOORS

PAIRED FRONT DOORS

SIX PANEL DOORS

FOUR PANE WINDOWS

TWELVE PANE WINDOWS

RAISED SURROUNDS ON CLASSICAL WINDOWS.

SINGLE STOREY BAY WINDOWS

BOW WINDOWS

FLEMISH BOND

DAMP COURSES AND RAISED FLOORS WITH VENTS INTRODUCED

STEEP PITCH ROOFS

GIANT COLUMNS ON LARGE TERRACES

STUCCOED WALLS

PLAIN CHIMNEYS

BOLD CORNICES

SHALLOW PITCH ROOFS

PAIRED AND TRIPLE ITALIANATE WINDOWS

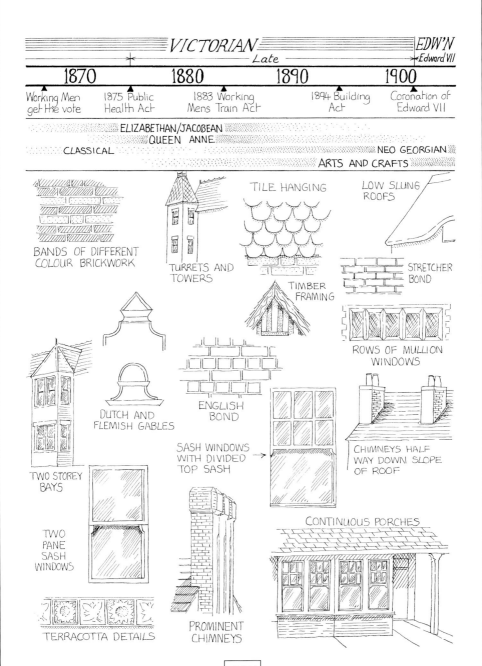

VICTORIAN
Late

EDW'N
→ Edward VII

1870	1880	1890	1900
Working Men get the vote	1875 Public Health Act	1883 Working Mens Train Act	1894 Building Act	Coronation of Edward VII

ELIZABETHAN/JACOBEAN
QUEEN ANNE
CLASSICAL
NEO GEORGIAN
ARTS AND CRAFTS

BANDS OF DIFFERENT COLOUR BRICKWORK

TURRETS AND TOWERS

TILE HANGING

TIMBER FRAMING

LOW SLUNG ROOFS

STRETCHER BOND

ROWS OF MULLION WINDOWS

DUTCH AND FLEMISH GABLES

ENGLISH BOND

SASH WINDOWS WITH DIVIDED TOP SASH

CHIMNEYS HALF WAY DOWN SLOPE OF ROOF

TWO STOREY BAYS

TWO PANE SASH WINDOWS

CONTINUOUS PORCHES

TERRACOTTA DETAILS

PROMINENT CHIMNEYS

PLACES TO VISIT

BLACK COUNTRY MUSEUM, Tipton Rd, Dudley, West Midlands (tel: 0121 557 9643; www.bclm.co.uk). Industrial village with Victorian back-to-backs, terraces, shops and chapel (although they are fitted out as they would have been in early 1900s). Very atmospheric with working features.

BEAMISH, THE NORTH OF ENGLAND OPEN AIR MUSEUM, Beamish, County Durham (tel: 01207 231811; www.beamish.org.uk).

BACK-TO-BACKS, Inge Street (next to Hippodrome Theatre), Birmingham (tel: 0121 666 7671, phone to book a visit as room is limited; www.nationaltrust.org.uk). Reconstruction of four back-to-backs complete with interior fittings, laundry room and privies.

CARLYLE'S HOUSE, 24 Cheyne Row, Chelsea, London SW3 (tel: 0207 352 7087; www.nationaltrust.org.uk). Victorian interiors in the house of the writer, Thomas Carlyle.

COGGES FARM MUSEUM, Church Lane, Cogges, Witney, Oxon (tel: 01993 772602). Good example of a Victorian farmhouse kitchen with working range.

IRONBRIDGE GORGE MUSEUMS, Ironbridge, Telford, Salop (tel: 01952 432166; www.ironbridge.org.uk). A collection of industrial sites with late 18th and 19th century houses at Blists Hill.

GEFFRYE MUSEUM, Kingsland Road, London E2 (tel: 0207 739 9893; www.Geffrye-museum.org.uk). Period interiors on display.

PORT SUNLIGHT, nr Birkenhead, The Wirral (www.portsunlight.org.uk). Exceptional late Victorian and Edwardian Arts and Crafts style houses.

SALTAIRE, north of Bradford (shop and information: 01274 774993; www.thisisbradford.co.uk).

SUNNYCROFT, 200 Holyhead Rd, Wellington, Telford, Salop (tel: 1952 242884; www.nationaltrust.org.uk).

VICTORIA AND ALBERT MUSEUM, Cromwell Road, London SW7 (www.vam.ac.uk). Collections of period furniture and interior fittings.

COUNTRY HOUSES: The following sites although not covered in this book (see *The Country House Explained*, Countryside Books) do contain Victorian rooms and fittings which may be relevant (NT, National Trust; EH, English Heritage): Audley End, Essex (NT), Brodsworth Hall, South Yorkshire (EH), Charlecote Park, Warwick (NT), Cragside, Northumberland (NT), Down House, Orpington, Kent (EH), Hughenden Manor, High Wycombe, Bucks (NT), Osborne House, Isle of Wight, (EH), Standen, East Grinstead, Sussex (NT), Waddesdon Manor, Aylesbury, Bucks (NT), Wightwick Manor, Wolverhampton (NT).

GENERAL INFORMATION

THE VICTORIAN SOCIETY, 1 Priory Gardens, London W4 1TT (tel: 0208 994 1019; www.victorian-society.org.uk). This is a registered charity dedicated to saving Victorian buildings and promoting a better understanding of them.

GLOSSARY

AEDICULE: The surrounding of a window or door by a raised moulding or pilasters with a form of pediment across the top. Common on Classically styled houses from the 1830s.

AREA: Common name for the open space in front of a large terraced house down which steps led to the basement.

ARCHITRAVE: The lowest section of the entablature. In this context it refers to the door surround.

ASHLAR: Smooth stone masonry with fine joints.

ASTYLAR: A façade with no vertical features, such as columns.

BALUSTER: Plain or decorated post supporting the stair rail.

BALUSTRADE: A row of decorated uprights (balusters) with a rail along the top.

BARGEBOARD: External vertical boards which protect the ends of the sloping roof on a gable and were often decorated.

BAY WINDOW: A window projecting from the façade of a house up a single or number of storeys, but always resting on the ground.

BONDING: The way bricks are laid in a wall with the different patterns formed by alternative arrangements of headers (the short ends) and stretchers (the long side).

CAPITAL: The decorated top of a Classical column.

CASEMENT: A window which is hinged along the side.

CHIMNEYPIECE: An internal fireplace surround.

CHIMNEYBREAST: The main body of the chimney, including the fireplace and flues.

COPING STONE: A protective capping running along the top of a wall.

CORNICE: The top section of the entablature, which in this context refers to the moulding which runs around the top of an external or internal wall.

COVING: A large concave moulding which covers the joint between the top of a wall and ceiling.

DADO: The base of a Classical column, which in this context refers to the bottom section of a wall between the skirting and dado or chair rail.

DORMER: An upright window set in the angle of the roof and casting light into the attic rooms.

EAVES: The section of the roof timbers under the tiles or slates where they either meet the wall (and a parapet continues above) or project over it (usually protected by a facia board which supports the guttering).

ENTABLATURE: The horizontal lintel supported by columns in a Classical temple.

FAÇADE: The main vertical face of the house.

FANLIGHT:	The window above a door lighting the hall beyond. Named after the radiating bars in semicircular Georgian and Regency versions.
FINIAL:	An ornamental piece on top of a railing or the end of the roof ridge.
FLUTING:	The vertical concave grooves running up a column or pilaster.
FRIEZE:	The middle section of the entablature, in this context referring to the section of the wall between the picture rail and cornice.
GABLE:	The pointed upper section of wall at the end of a pitched roof.
GLAZING BARS:	The internal divisions of a window which support the panes.
HEARTH:	The stone or brick base of a fireplace.
JAMBS:	The sides of an opening for a door or window.
KEYSTONE:	The top stone in an arch, often projected as a feature.
LINTEL:	A flat beam which is fitted above a door or window to take the load of the wall above.
MOULDING:	A decorative strip of wood, stone or plaster.
MULLION:	A vertical member dividing a window.
ORIEL:	A projecting window supported from the wall rather than the ground.
PARAPET:	The top section of wall which continues above the sloping end of the roof.
PARGETING:	A raised pattern formed from plaster on an external wall (popular originally in the East of England).
PEDIMENT:	A low-pitched triangular feature supported by columns or pilasters above a Classically styled door or window in this context.
PILASTER:	A flat Classical column fixed to a wall or fireplace and projecting slightly from it.
PITCH:	The angle by which a roof slopes. A plain sloping roof of two sides is called a pitched roof.
QUOIN:	The corner stones at the junction of walls. Often raised above the surface, made from contrasting materials or finished differently from the rest of the wall for decorative effect.
RENDER:	A protective covering for a wall.
REVEAL:	The sides (jambs) of a recessed window or door opening.
RUSTICATION:	The cutting of stone or moulding of stucco into blocks separated by deep incised lines, sometimes with a rough hewn finish. Often used to highlight the base of a Classically styled house.
SASH WINDOW:	A window of two separate sashes which slide vertically (or horizontally on smaller Yorkshire sash windows).
SKIRTING:	The protective strip of wood at the base of a wall.

STRING: The side support panel for a stair.
STRING COURSE: A horizontal band running across a façade and usually projecting.
STUCCO: A plaster which was used to render, imitate stonework and form decorative features especially on Classical styled houses.
TRACERY: The ribs which divide the top of a stone window and are formed into patterns.
TRANSOM: The horizontal bar in a window.
VERNACULAR: Buildings made from local materials in styles and methods of construction passed down within a distinct area, as opposed to architect-designed structures made from mass produced materials.
VOUSSOIR: The wedge-shaped stones or bricks which make up an arch.

INDEX